The World of
ALEXANDER-KINS

Patricia R. Smith

COLLECTOR BOOKS
A Division of Schroeder Publishing Co., Inc.

The current values in this book should be used only as a guide. They are not intended to set prices, which vary from one section of the country to another. Auction prices as well as dealer prices vary greatly and are affected by condition as well as demand. Neither the Author nor the Publisher assumes responsibility for any losses that might be incurred as a result of consulting this guide.

Cover: "Wendy Loves Swimming" #406-1955. Courtesy Florence Phelps.

Sand Castle by Nipigon Studios, Inc.

Approved by the Madame Alexander Doll Company
Editors: Beverly Harrington, Debbie Harrington

DEDICATION

This volume is dedicated to Madame Beatrice Alexander because she chose to share her talents with the world through beautifully designed and dressed dolls. She never forgot how attached children become to their dolls and she used this method to instruct and inspire youngsters by "bringing alive" paintings, fiction, great plays and movies through her dolls. Wendy Ann/Alexander-kins gave the child a playmate with a wardrobe. Here again, Madame Alexander's exceptional skills as a designer were outstanding, as these miniature dolls continue to be the best dressed and best loved in the world.

MADAME ALEXANDER
by
Debbie Harrington

May 1, 1984 was a beautiful day as Madame Beatrice Alexander was shown into the cabinet chambers of the State Capital building in Tallahassee, Florida. Awaiting her arrival was Governor Bob Graham and his cabinet.

A resolution was introduced and passed by Secretary of State, George Firestone, and the cabinet to honor Madame Alexander for the great contributions she has made to her profession and her most generous support of the Museum of Florida History. A large, lengthy scroll was presented to Madame Alexander by Governor Graham.

This was yet another honor added to a vast list of tributes paid to Madame Alexander for her remarkable accomplishments within the doll profession and for her contributions to the betterment of the world through her many and varied charities. Madame Alexander believes that each human being adds or detracts from the world by his presence. Those who add to the world give of themselves by their God-given talents and abilities to help others through advice, counsel and actions. The ones that detract take only for themselves.

Madame Alexander's dolls have always held a position of esteem in modern doll collections throughout the United States. More collectors are entering the field each and every day. These collectors have the opportunity to be with Madame Aleaxander once a year at Disneyworld in Florida. When the tickets for the dinner with Madame Alexander go on sale at Disneyworld, the phoned-in orders actually tie up the trunk lines into Orlando. The incoming calls and attempted calls amount to over 5,000. This affair has become Madame Alexander's way of saying "thank you" to her admirers and collectors and to those who appreciate her life-long efforts to make nothing but the finest quality dolls.

(The history and background on Madame Alexander can be found on pages 1-3 of *Madame Alexander Collector's Dolls,* Vol. 1.)

CREDITS

We would like to thank the following collectors for caring and sharing dolls from their collections. We are only sorry that we could not use every photograph taken or sent, but space was just not available.

Name withheld by request - photos by Richard Olsen of Roosevelt-Baker Photo
   Co., Houston, TX
Author's photos - by Dwight F. Smith
Gene Beckman - photos by Gene and Wilson Graham
Shirley Bertrand - photos by Dwight F. Smith
Elinor Bibby - photos by Dr. Douglas Bibby
Kathy Bookstein - photos by Dwight F. Smith
Vivian Brady - photos by Vivian Brady
Joanna Brunken - photos by Margaret Mandel
Nancy Celletti - photos by Nancy Celletti
Jean Couch - photos by Jean Couch
Sandra Crane - photos by Vivian Brady
Jan Cravens - photos by Dwight F. Smith
Linda Crowsey - photos by Dwight F. Smith
LaDonna Dolan - photos by Ted Long
Gary Green - photos by Dwight F. Smith
Sharon Griffiths - photos by Dwight F. Smith
Gloria Harris - photos by Dwight F. Smith
Bernice Heister - photos by Bernice Heister
Shirley Kronkowski - photos by Dwight F. Smith
Roberta Lago - photos by Ted Long
Margaret Mandel - photos by Margaret Mandel
Billie McCabe - photos by Dwight F. Smith
Christine McWilliams - photos by Dwight F. Smith
Florence Phelps - photos by Dwight F. Smith and "Flip" Phelps
Doris Richardson - photos by Brenda Richardson
Lillian Roth - photos by Dwight F. Smith and sons, Nader and Ramin Modabber
Cathy Ruggiero - photos by Margaret Mandel
Pat Timmons - photos by Chester Berkley
Karen Vincent - photos by Dwight F. Smith
Jeannie Wilson - photos by Jeannie Wilson
Loramay Wilson - photos by Loramay Wilson

CONTENTS

THE WORLD OF ALEXANDER-KINS

In 1953 Madame Alexander, by popular demand, once again created for the children of America, her inimitable miniature dolls, worthy of being placed amongst cherished porcelains.

All the same fine craftsmanship, the same beauty of design, the same excellent fabrics, and the same integrity that have made Madame Alexander a famous name wherever beautiful dolls are sold, went into the making of these little dolls so affectionately called the Wendy Alexander-kins.

Wendy Ann had the most beautiful and varied wardrobe ever designed for a miniature doll. In 1953 and 1954 a little doll called "Quiz-kin", with push buttons on the back to make the head move from side to side or up and down, also came with an extensive wardrobe.

The name ALEXANDER-KINS refers to all the 7½"-8" all hard plastic dolls, such as Little Women, Quiz-kins, Maggie Mix-up and Wendy Ann, later called Wendy/Wendy-kins.

Wendy Ann miniature dolls came in several catagories, such as Wendy Likes To Make Believe as a Ballerina, Bride and Groom, Being a Queen, Dancing, A Majorette, An Old Fashioned Girl, A Bridesmaid or even A Rose Fairy. Wendy faced her real world in school clothes, outfits to go shopping in, to go to Sunday School, a dude ranch, a circus or a rodeo. Wendy reflected the wonders of reading through storybook characters such as Romeo and Juliet, Guardian Angel, Scarlett O'Hara, Cinderella or Hansel and Gretel. Wendy had a complete wardrobe of party clothes, and special occasion clothes such as Maypole dance, dressed as Aunts or Cousins, as a minister, a governess or even as twins. Wendy sport clothes included skaters, sunsuits, riding outfits or tennis clothes. Wendy had coats and suits for every occasion, furniture, a teaset and even her own trousseaus and trunks. Wendy Ann was an all-around American Girl!

Although the present Little Women still bear the Alexander-kins tag, the name was dropped in 1963 and until the end of production of the non-International 8" dolls in 1965, the Wendy-kins tag was used.

Chronology Of The 7½"-8" Dolls

1953: 7½". Straight-leg non-walker, solid, heavy hard plastic. Shorter looking face, excellent face color, skin tones slightly tan color. MARKS: "Alex." on back. TAGS: Alexander-kins, Madame Alexander, etc, or Quiz-kin.

1954: 7½" and 8". Most straight-leg non-walkers, but some straight-leg walkers. Lighter in weight, more hollow and not as solid. Softer color flesh tones, head design slightly altered. MARKS: "Alex." on back. TAGS: Alexander-kins, Madame Alexander, etc., Quiz-kin.

1955: 8". All are straight-leg walkers. MARKS: same as 1954.

1956: Most bend-knee walkers, but some straight-leg walkers. MARKS: "Alex." on back. TAGS: Alexander-kin, name of character, or Madame Alexander, etc.

1957: Bend-knee walkers. MARKS: same as 1956.

1958: Bend-knee walkers. MARKS: same as 1957.

1959: Bend-knee walkers. MARKS: same as 1958.

1960: Bend-knee walkers. MARKS: same as 1959.

1961: Bend-knee walkers. MARKS: Same as 1960.

1962: Bend-knee walkers. MARKS: Same as 1961.

1963: Bend-knee walkers. MARKS: "Alex." on back. TAGS: Wendy-kins, Madame Alexander, etc., or name of character.

1964: Bend-knee walkers. MARKS: same as 1963.

1965: Bend-knee walkers with a few bend-knee non-walkers. Last year of Wendy-kin clothes. MARKS: same as 1964.

1966: Bend-knee non-walkers. 8" dolls used for Storyland, Internationals and Americana dolls. Ballerina and Bride.

1967 to 1969: Bend-knee walkers. Used for Storyland, Internationals and Americana dolls. Ballerinas and Brides.

1970: Bend-knee walkers. Dolls used for Storyland, Internationals, Ballerina and Bride.

1971: Same as 1970.

1972: Bend-knee non-walkers. Dolls used for Storyland, Internationals, Disney's Snow White and Alice in Wonderland.

1973: Most are straight-leg non-walkers, but few are bend-knee non-walkers. Eyes are much wider in this mold change, eyebrows painted darker and the whites of the eyes show at bottom of pupil. The cheeks are rosy and skin tones are flesh-toned. Dolls used for Storyland, Internationals, Ballerina and Bride. MARKS: "Alex." on back. TAGS: Alexander-kin or Madame Alexander, etc. name of character.

1974: Straight-leg non-walkers. Dolls used for Storyland and Internationals, Ballerina and Bride. MARKS: same as 1973.

1975: Straight-leg non-walkers. Dolls used for Storyland, Internationals, Ballerina and Bride. The end of 1975 also saw the end of the use of detachable jewelery because of new government regulations on safety for children. MARKS: Same as 1974.

1976: Straight-leg non-walkers. Dolls used for Storyland and Internationals, Ballerina and Bride. Marks: "Alex." on back. TAGS: same as 1975.

1977 to 1981: Some of the Alex. marked straight-leg non-walkers still available, but most have been changed to the ALEXANDER marked bodies that have powdery, chalky skin tones and high cheek color. The dark skin dolls have fuller cheeks and a rounder face. All are straight-leg non-walkers. MARKS: "Alexander" on backs. TAG: Madame Alexander, name of character.

1982 to date: Straight-leg non-walkers. Mouth in this new mold change has deep indentations over the upper lip that casts a shadow as the doll is looked at straight-on and makes her appear as if she has a mustache. Doll has chalky, powdery body and almost white skin tones. MARKS: "Alexander" on backs. TAGS: Madame Alexander. etc., name of character.

General Information

Although the Alexander-kins were introduced in 1953, the actual production time of these first dolls, as all others, is relatively shorter than a year. Each year the doll and toy industry has a "Toy Fair" in New York City in February. Many buyers go to see the new production items, place orders and get to know the manufacturers better. Also, during the Spring and Summer, there are smaller Trade Shows around the country in places such as Dallas, Chicago, Atlanta, and Los Angeles, where buyers can go to place orders and re-order, but they do not get to see the entire lines from each maker in person, and must use catalogs. These Regional shows are on a much smaller scale than the New York Toy Fair. After the orders are placed it takes several months for the new items to reach the stores. We must realize that the doll and toy industry has always been orientated towards "seasons", such as Christmas (generally 45% to 65% of their total business), Summer-related merchandise, Easter, Halloween, etc. and their production is planned towards these times. Orders placed in February usually begin to arrive at the stores in May to August, and some not until October and November. Generally, factories stop taking new or re-orders around the last of October or first weeks of November. This allows them to complete all that year's orders before they begin on the up-coming year's production. One factory shuts down the entire month of December and all employees take their vacation during this "change over" time.

Since there is a cycle to the introduction of dolls, we should realize that dolls are carried over from one year into the next, plus, up until a very few years ago, most stores carried over unsold stock (many still do). Then, take the child that received an Alexander-kin for Christmas of 1953 and the parents, aunts, grandmothers and friend purchased other clothing items for this doll during the following year for such occasions as a Birthday, Easter, etc. So it should not be a surprise that a certain doll had clothes from a year later. Madame Alexander dolls have always been higher priced due to the fine quality and are found in the finer stores. Not every parent could afford to purchase these dolls, but the ones that did usually added wardrobe items by buying separately boxed clothing or making clothing for the dolls themselves rather than purchasing another dressed doll. One can see why the played-with dolls can have on a variety of clothing that may not be correct for the year the doll was made.

The market for the Alexander-kins increased each year after their introduction in 1953 until the peak years of production which were 1955 to 1957. After 1957 they began to decrease until they ceased altogether in 1965.

Buying And Building An Alexander-Kins Collection

First, you must study the subject! See and feel as many of the dolls as you can. Learn the years of production for certain dolls, such as the straight-leg non-walker of 1953, and when and how many years the bend-knee walkers were produced. Study the various styles and materials used for the dolls for these different years. The main thing is to become well acquainted with the dolls through books and especially the Alexander Company catalogs reprints, which can be ordered from the addresses following. Be sure to send a self-addressed, stamped envelope to ask for the prices of the catalogs:

Jane Thomas, Old Town Doll & Toy Emporium, 2611 San Diego Ave., San Diego, CA 92110
Barbara Jo's Dolls, P.O. Box 1481, Brockton, MA 02402

Not all of the dolls/clothing are shown in these catalogs, nor the variations of the outfits, but hundreds are shown. There are variations in design and materials used for many different outfits, but be sure these are true variations and not something made-up for the doll.

Madame Alexander used cloth tags in her clothing except in a couple of areas, such as if there was more than one piece to the outfit, like a coat and matching dress, only the coat or the dress may be tagged. The Hawaiian does not have a tag. You must be aware that other companies used clothing tags, companies like Vogue Dolls and Ideal Dolls. So if a tag has been cut out and only a tiny bit remains it does not mean that the item was made by Madame Alexander, it could belong to another company. In relation to tags, it must be noted that tags are known to have been reproduced. Tags on Madame Alexander clothes can be sewn in a variety of places, like the back seam of the dress, over the collar or under the collar, sewn at the same time as the seam (single row of stitches) or within the seam and under the garment snaps. The way the tags are attached varies also, for some were put on when the snaps were sewn and these snaps and tags will be sewn on two sides of the snap only by machine (not on all four sides as home seamstresses are prone to do). Some of the tags are sewn on with the same machine stitches as the sewing of the dress and some have machine single stitches over and over in the middle of the tag.

The Madame Alexander clothing is known for the use of square snap closures, but other companies used square snaps also, such as Arranbee and American Character. Square snaps can still be purchased and are used on production dolls currently on the market that are not Madame Alexander dolls. Again, the Alexander clothes snaps are sewn on two sides and not all four sides.

There are reproduction clothes on the market and have been for a few years. Some are excellent quality and others can be detected easily. Check for correct fit to the doll, the overall effect of the clothes and the doll, and the materials used. Look to see if everything, including laces and trim, are in scale to the outfit. You must remember that Madame Alexander used only the finest of materials, trims and laces. It is important to get to know the older materials versus the new ones. Mainly, it takes study and experience to be even slightly certain about the clothing.

In 1953, 1954, and 1955, the socks used on the Alexander-kins were a heavy weave, soft and are folded to the inside at the tops. These socks are just like the ones found on the Vogue ''Ginny'' dolls and others of this period. The socks used from 1956 to 1965 are closely knit nylon, smooth and silky with very fine ribbing. The first few years, the Alexander-kin shoes were stitched all the way round the top of the shoes and have fuzzy-feeling soles.

There are certain hairstyles that are correct for a given doll, such as the Juliet doll. A catalog reprint may picture a certain outfit on a doll with a flip hairstyle or pigtails, and it would be nice to think we could all have the correct doll, hairstyle and dress on one doll, but unless found completely unplayed with, the odds are against it. There was an overlapping from year to year on doll styles and in clothing, plus these dolls were really a wonderful play doll and generally were not put up for viewing as they are today. The only thing that we must be concerned about is overpricing on a doll without ''correct'' clothes for the year of the doll. You would expect to pay much more for a 1953 doll in a mint 1953 outfit than a 1953 doll in a mint 1957 outfit. But, if the price is right, it certainly is alright to buy the doll, watch for a 1953 outfit and a 1957 doll and change their clothes to have two correct dolls.

There are a few things that decrease the price of these played-with dolls. One is if the dress has been washed and the original sizing has been removed, and if items are missing such as hats, wooden toys, dogs, purses, crowns, etc. Hats can be a *big* problem. It is most difficult to determine if the hat may be correct or not, as there are a vast amount of variations other than those shown in the catalog reprints. Hats seemed to get lost easily and Alexander hats are not marked nor tagged and other companies used the same styles and materials. Here again, it must be noted that Madame Alexander used extremely fine quality materials and workmanship, and these materials were in scale to the style of the hat and the style of the period in which the dolls were made. The natural, nylon/rayon straw used on hats were of fine quality and woven and in scale, not large rows ending with a cut-off place in the back. The chin straps when used, were attached with a small brad and not just punched through the hat with a metal piece showing on the top side. The old hats are almost impossible to reproduce as old materials, in scale, are very hard to find.

Remember, experience is still the best teacher. Look at all the Alexander-kins you can and try to remember the details of each of the clothing items. You will notice things like the 1953 and 1954, and some 1955 dresses are longer than the later ones, the soles of the first few years shoes are like suede where later ones are slick. You will see the early dolls had heavy ribbed socks and later ones the fine, smooth and slightly ribbed ones. The straw and rayon/nylon straw on the hats are single stitched rows and soft, not over sized per row. You will see how the lace pattern is always in scale to the outfit. You will get to know the quality of the workmanship of sewing each and every seam and you will be able to detect repairs and additions. Time and experience will sharpen your instincts so that you become aware what years the bend-knee walker was made so that you will not buy a re-dressed International or Storybook doll as an Alexander-kin. You will become aware that there are no brown-eyed Alexander-kins.

If you are looking at a doll and you have a good overall feeling about that doll and the price is right, go ahead and buy it, but if you have any doubts, do not buy it as you most likely will never be happy with that particular doll. Buy through a reliable dealer for best quality, but is it fun to buy . . . carefully . . . at auctions, flea markets and out-of-the-way shops. The main thing is for you to have fun with your hobby of collecting the adorable Alexander-kins.

11" "Candy Kid" using the original "Wendy Ann" mold in composition in the late 1930's. Many are tagged "Wendy Ann" as well as being marked with the name on the body. Some have swivel waists, and they came with sleep eyes and also with painted eyes. The "Wendy Ann" came with an extensive and extremely fine quality wardrobe which was also used for such varied dolls as: Alice in Wonderland, Cinderella, Ballerina, Scarlett O'Hara and a great many others. Courtesy Jean Couch.

The "Wendy Ann" face has a sweet and innocent look and adapted well to a little girl doll, and also as character dolls such as Cinderella, Scarlett and many others. The quality of the composition and all clothes made for the doll was exceptional. (Author).

The "Wendy Ann Alexander-kins" were sold each year as a basic doll with panties and socks and shoes. Almost all the outfits made for the 7½"-8" dolls were sold and packaged separately so a personal wardrobe could be purchased for any child. Courtesy Pat Timmons.

Left: 7½″ straight-leg non-walker of 1953 and 1954. Tan flesh tones, heavy in weight. They eyes are oval and the lips are dark red. Right: 8″ straight-leg walker of 1955. Lighter flesh tones and slightly lighter lip color. This doll can get shiny with play and have a bisque look. Both are marked "Alex." on backs.

Left: Bend-knee walker made from 1956 to 1965. Basically same doll as the straight-leg walker, but has the bend knees. Right: Bend-knee non-walker has pink flesh tones. The closer the dolls were made to end of their production in 1972 the more pronounced the lower lashes were painted and the more "powdery" the bodies became. This 4th doll in the series was made from 1964 to 1972. Both are marked "Alex." on their backs.

Left: The 5th doll in the series became a straight-leg non-walker and was made from 1973 to 1976. They have vivid pink flesh tones, very round eyes with the whites showing below the eyes and lips are more orange in color. They are marked "Alex." on backs. Right: 1977 to date are the extremely pale pink flesh color, straight-leg non-walkers with eyes now back to more like the original dolls. Mouths are modeled with a look of a mustache over upper lip with a smaller area of the lips painted. Dolls are marked with the full name "Alexander" on the backs.

Full face view of #1, straight-leg non-walker and #2 straight-leg walker.

Full face of #3 bend-knee walker and #4 bend-knees only.

Full face view of #5 straight-leg non-walker marked ''Alex.'' and the #6 straight-leg non-walker marked ''Alexander.''

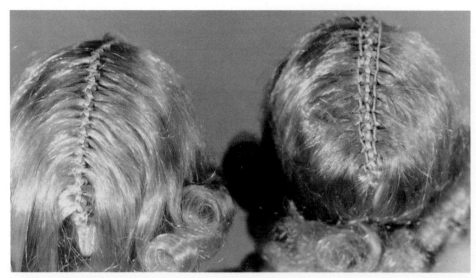

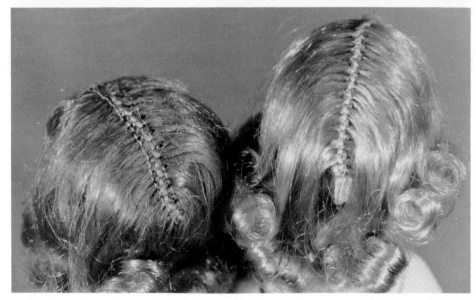

The early 7½″-8″ dolls have wigs that are stitched down each side of the center seam. These wigs were used on the straight-leg non-walkers of 1953-1954 and the straight-leg walkers of 1955. They were also used on the bend-knee walkers, but so were the other style stitched wigs. Shown are a straight-leg walker and a bend-knee walker.

The later stitching is shown on a straight-leg non-walker with "Alex." on the back. This same style is used today on current dolls. With the introduction of the #5 doll (straight-leg, "Alex" mold) the hair used on the wigs was of a finer, silkier material.

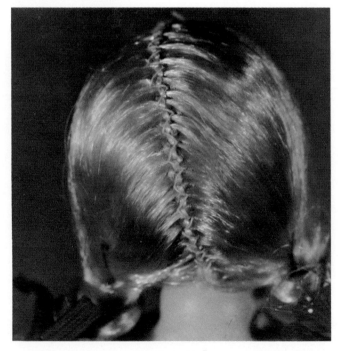

"Little Southern Girl", #305-1953. Straight-leg non-walker. Gown is three-fourths length and she wears matching pantaloons. Tag: Alexander-kin, also came tagged: Madame Alexander, etc. On the right is "Garden Party" #488-1955. Courtesy Gene Beckman.

"Apple Annie of Broadway", 1953-1954. Can be straight-leg non-walker or straight-leg walker. Has special hairdo. Collar can also be a lace trimmed "Peter Pan" style, and gown can have lace attached to hem line. Courtesy Gary Green.

"Agatha", 1953. Straight-leg non-walker. Jacket ties in front. Has lace-trimmed pantaloons. Tag: Alexander-kin. Can also be tagged: "Agatha", and "Madame Alexander, etc." Courtesy Bernice Heister.

"Little Victoria", #376-1953. Mint, all original. Tagged Alexander-kin. Straight-leg non-walker. Courtesy LaDonna Dolan.

"Country Picnic", #376-1953. Straight-leg non-walker. Cotton gown and white jacket ties in front and has eyelet lace trim. She wears organdy pantaloons with lace trim. Tag: Alexander-kin. Courtesy Marge Meisinger.

"Wendy Ann", 1953. Straight-leg non-walker in cardboard dresser with accessories: pink curlers, towels, blue hangers, white straw hat with pink roses, hankie, basket, pink nightie, blue and white polka-dot dress. Hair in braids with yellow ribbon and flowers. Tag: Alexander-kins. Courtesy Margaret Mandel.

"Little Madaline", 1953. Straight-leg non-walker. Name inspired by Ludwig Bemelman's stories. Has long cotton pantaloons. Dress matches larger doll. Tag: Alexander-kin. The back side of bonnet is same material as dress. Courtesy Marge Meisinger.

"Quiz-kin" Bride and Groom, 1953. Straight-leg non-walker. The Bride is patterned after "Wendy Bride" in the 15" and 18" size of 1953. "Bridesmaid", 1953. Straight-leg non-walker. Flowers were added. Bride and Groom are tagged: Quiz-kin and Bridesmaid: Alexander-kin. Courtesy Gene Beckman.

"Easter", 1953. Straight-leg non-walker. Organdy sundress trimmed with lace and braid. Sundress wraps around and ties through metal eyelets in back and is formed for lace panties to show. Bonnet is embroidered doily style in back and sides are starched heavy net with tatting style edging around front. Lavender bow on top. Came in yellow, blue, and pink. Alexander-kins wrist with "I Am Wendy Ann" on inside of tag. Carries basket with chicken and small plastic tennis racket. Courtesy Christine McWilliams.

"Easter", 1953. Has two rows of lace at hem of organdy dress. Pink satin sash. Same style hat as used on the other doll, but has pink ribbon. Straight-leg non-walker. Large basket added. Tag: Alexander-kin. Courtesy Florence Phelps.

"Little Edwardian", #415-1953-1955. Can be on a straight-leg non-walker or a straight-leg walker. Tag: Alexander-kin. Can be white dots or stars on a blue background. Left: Courtesy Lillian Roth (polka dots). Right: Courtesy Vivian Brady (stars).

"Peter Pan Quiz-kin". Jersey pants with rest of costume made of felt with leatherette belt. Came with red and blonde caracul wig over molded hair. Has two buttons on back to move head. Tag: Alexander-kin. Courtesy Bernice Heister.

"Quiz-kin", 1953. Straight-leg non-walker. Dress has no snaps and wraps around waist to tie in front. Two push buttons on back to make head move. Tag: Quiz-kin. Courtesy Marge Meisinger.

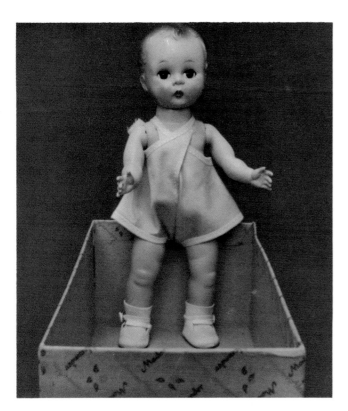

"Quiz-kin", #312-1953. Straight-leg non-walker. Push buttons on back. Straps cross and tie in back. Tag: Quiz-kin. Courtesy Pat Timmons.

"Quiz-kin", #312-1953. Straight-leg non-walker. Push buttons on back to make head move. Straps cross in back and tie. Tag: Quiz-kins. Matching bonnet. Courtesy Christine McWilliams.

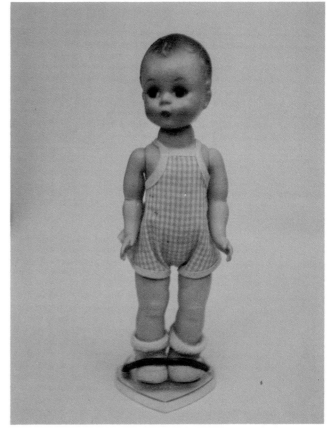

"Quiz-kins", 1953-1954. Straight-leg non-walkers. Push buttons on back to make head move. Molded hair and wigged over molded hair. Rompers came in variation of prints. Left: Courtesy Florence Phelps. Right: Courtesy Vivian Brady.

"Quiz-kin" in yet another variation of sunsuit with different print. Straight-leg non-walker. Has button in back to make head move. Came with molded hair and as shown, molded hair under wig. Courtesy Elinor Bibby.

"Quiz-kin", 1953. In original playsuit with matching bonnet. This outfit was available in 1953 and 1954 in various colors, with and without the bonnet, and with and without a short sleeve bodysuit. Also came in blue with red and white trim. Courtesy Elinor Bibby.

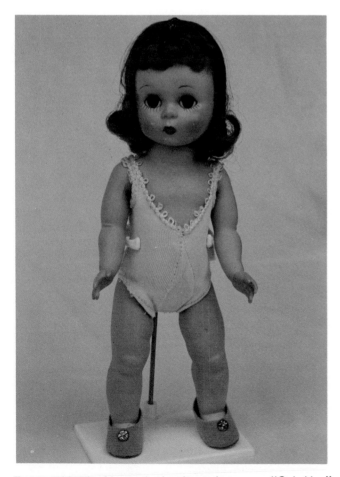

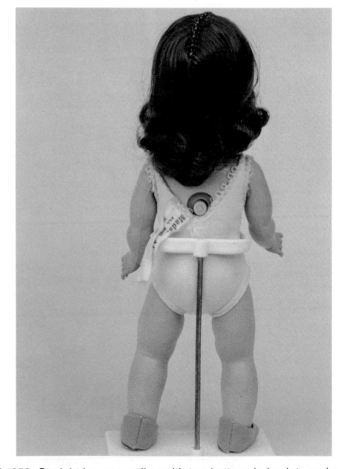

Front and back of jersey bodysuit used on some "Quiz-kins" of 1953. Straight-leg non-walker with two buttons in back to make head move. Replaced shoes. Note detail of seaming in center, from front to back. Courtesy Florence Phelps.

Left: "School Outfit", 1953-1954. Straight-leg non-walker with very unusual hairdo for the year. Taffeta dress, pinafore ties in back through metal eyelets. Right: "Wendy Looks As Sweet As A Lollipop", #326-1957. Polished cotton dress with rickrack trim. Had felt bonnet with flowers on top. Bend-knee walker. Tag: Alexander-kin. Courtesy Joanna Brunken.

"School Outfit", 1953-1954. Straight-leg non-walker. Polished cotton dress and cotton pinafore with matching bonnet. Tag: Alexander-kin. Courtesy Jay Minter.

"School Outfit", 1953-1954. Straight-leg non-walker. Polished cotton dress with lace trim and floral print polished cotton pinafore, which ties in back through metal eyelets. Straw hat with flowers. Courtesy Jeannie Wilson.

Dress and pinafore from 1953-1954. Straight-leg non-walker. Dress is cotton and pinafore is organdy. Replaced shoes and socks. May have had hat or bonnet. Tag: Alexander-kin. Courtesy Jay Minter.

"Wendy's Favorite Outfit", #342-1953. Straight-leg non-walker. Edges of sleeves same as pinafore. Came in other colors also. Red flowers and ribbon on hat. Tag: Alexander-kin. Courtesy Vivian Brady.

1953-1954 Jumper outfit with one-piece bloomers attached to organdy blouse under the jumper. This same outfit also came with pink stripes and rickrack trim. Replaced shoes and socks. Jumper buttons down the back. Hat may have come on this doll. Courtesy Florence Phelps.

1953-1954 Jumper with one-piece blouse and bloomers. Original starched lace hat. Buttons down back. Tag: Alexander-kins. Courtesy Jay Minter.

The black flowered pinafore outfits were made from 1953 through 1956. The first was used on the composition "Wendy Ann" in the late 1930's. (See "The Most Beautiful Dolls" by Jane Ruggles Thomas, page 46). The dresses came in a variation of colors and materials such as waffle pique and cotton. Tag: Alexander-kin. Left photo: The doll on the right is an early one and the hat looks more like the original in catalogs. Courtesy Florence Phelps. Dolls in left photo have replaced shoes and socks. Right photo: Pique dress, hat may not be original. Courtesy Gary Green.

Early 1953 or 1954 pinafore outfit. The dress is waffle pique and the pinafore is cotton using different color floral print. Hat is missing. Tag: Alexander-kin. Courtesy Jay Minter.

1953-1954 Jumper of taffeta with matching bonnet and with taffeta bloomers attached to organdy blouse. Outfit could be worn together or separately. Replaced shoes and socks. Tag: Alexander-kin. This same jumper and blouse/bloomers also came in pink/white check and used in an F.A.O. Schwarz exclusive as "Wendy Trouseau" in 1953. See *Madame Alexander Collector's Dolls, Series II*, page 6. (Author)

1953-1954 straight-leg non-walker in organdy dress and apron, ribbons in hair. This outfit also came with a plain straw hat with red ribbon around the brim and streamers down the back. The shape of hat is like "Dude Ranch", #449-1955. Courtesy Jay Minter.

Organdy panties with three rows of lace that matches the lace on the dress and apron. The owner has two dolls in same outfit and photos of each were taken using the best here, so one doll has white shoes and other has black shoes. Courtesy Jay Minter.

"Ballerina", 1954. Is on wrong doll, which should be a straight-leg walker. Costume is of satin and net with rhinestones. Matches larger ballerinas in the 15″ and 18″ sizes. Courtesy Sandra Crane.

Jumper dress with one-piece organdy blouse attached to bloomers of the same color and material as the dress. Tag: Alexander-kin. Can be straight-leg non-walker or straight-leg walker. Replaced shoes and socks. Courtesy Jay Minter.

1953-1954 outfit that also came in other materials. Cotton blouse attached to cotton bloomers under jumper dress which buttons down the back. They could be worn together or alone. Tagged Alexander-kin. Courtesy Elizabeth Montesano of Yesterday's Children.

Jumper removed so the one-piece romper and attached blouse can be seen. Courtesy Elizabeth Montesano of Yesterday's Children.

1953 straight-leg non-walker in pastel blue organdy, original shoes and socks. Bonnet is original to doll and is soft black velvet with lining of pink satin and pink plume. Doll may have had soft black velvet coat to match the bonnet. 1953. Tag: Alexander-kin. (Author)

1953 straight-leg non-walker shown in same dress as the organdy one with black/pink bonnet, but this dress is made of taffeta. Replaced shoes. Tagged: Alexander-kin. Came in various colors and is #459. Courtesy Gloria Harris.

1953, 1954

1953 straight-leg non-walker in pink organdy dress that may have had a coat and bonnet. Replaced hat. Courtesy Gloria Harris.

"Victoria", #0030C 1954. From the "Me and My Shadow Series", 1954. Straight-leg walker. Very elaborate gown that matches a larger doll. Tag: Can either be Alexander-kin or the Madame Alexander tag. Courtesy Bernice Heister.

"Mary Louise", 1954. Straight-leg walker. From the "Me and My Shadow Series", 1954. Dressed in Godey period costume and matches the larger 18″ size doll. #0035D in the series. Courtesy Gary Green.

"Garden Party", #347. Three-quarter length pink cotton dress with organdy pinafore that buttons down the back. Wears matching lace pantaloons. Pink flowers attached to sides of crocheted bandeau that is tied with pink ribbon. The ponytails were originally tied with tiny pink bows. Tag: Alexander-kin. Courtesy Jay Minter.

"Queen Elizabeth", 1954 #597 and #0030A from the "Me and My Shadow Series" (has matching Margaret face Queen wearing same gown and has white orlan ermine cape). Straight-leg walker. Wears brocade gown, sash with "jewel", has crown of five silver leaves attached to plastic with "diamonds" on front side of three leaves. Tag: Alexander-kins. The purple cape has attached orlan short cape which can tie around neck and others may be held over the upper arms with gold braid. Has gold tie shoes. The gown can be ivory or white in color, the sash can be blue or pale lavender, and there can be a variation of "jewels". The 1954 "Queen" is unique in that she is the only one that has the orlan cape attached to purple robe. Photo by Richard Olsen of Roosevelt-Baker Photo Co.

"So Dressed Up", 1954. 15″ "Binnie Walker" and her shadow "Wendy Ann". There is also a matching "Binnie" in sizes 18″ and 25″. Dresses are taffeta and hats are velvet. The "Wendy Ann" has very bright red wig and is tagged: Alexander-kin. The 15″ doll is tagged "Binnie Walker". (Author)

"Queen Elizabeth", #597 and #0030A from "Me and My Shadow Series", 1954. This view shows the crown with silver leaves attached to plastic ring. In attendance: an English Guard with a Scottish brigade. Courtesy Margaret Mandel.

"Quiz-kin" Bride, 1953 and Groom, 1954. Same dolls in 1954 except the Groom has caracul wig. The Bride matches the 1953 and 1954 larger Brides which came in 15″ and 18″ and have the "Margaret" face. Both dolls are straight-leg non-walkers and have push buttons in back to move head. Courtesy Lillian Roth.

"Little Godey", 1954. Jacket has black beading design and bonnet is cut out to thread chin ties. Tag: Alexander-kin, also found tagged: Madame Alexander. Courtesy Bernice Heister.

"Blue Danube", #351-1954. Straight-leg walker. Can also be on a straight-leg non-walker. From this angle the hat can be seen as well as the green netting over the muff. Tag: Alexander-kin. Courtesy Florence Phelps.

"Day in the Country", #350-1954. Straight-leg walker. Tagged: Alexander-kin. Photo by Richard Olsen of Roosevelt-Baker Photo Co.

"Little Victoria", #328-1954. Straight-leg walker. There are variations of the hat, but all have large pink flowers. The dress matches larger "Binnie Walker" short dress in 15"-#1524, 18"-#1824 and 25"-#2524 of 1954. The Binnie Walker dolls have braids and an open weave hat. Courtesy Vivian Brady.

"Little Victoria", #328-1954. Shows one of the variations of the hat. Courtesy Bernice Heister.

"Little Victoria", #328-1954. Straight-leg walker with a bonnet cut in one piece and held together with a brad in the back. Ties under the chin. She is shown with a ceramic figurine made in Japan, that sits on top of a revolving music box and uses one of the variations of hats. (Courtesy Marge Meisinger). (Author)

The back side of the bonnet on the "Little Victoria" of 1954. Tag: Alexander-kin, on dress. This style hat has been found on a Betsy McCall, but the material is a poor quality suedine and the flowers were missing. It is not known if the hat found was original to the Betsy McCall. (Author)

"Southern Belle" type of 1954. Beautifully detailed sleeves with small rows of tucking, straw bonnet with flowers on the sides. This same doll is also found with a crocheted style bonnet with flowers on the upper left hand side. Courtesy Christine McWilliams.

"Guardian Angel", #480-1954. Straight-leg walker. Multi-layered white wings, gold halo attached to clear plastic ring that is cut to head opening so it fits on the back of the head, and held on by chin strap. Metal star brads on gown and carries gold and silver harp. Wears silver tie slippers. Tag: Guardian Angel/Madame Alexander/Reg. U.S. Pat. Off./New York, N.Y. Courtesy Roberta Lago.

"Guardian Angel", #480-1954. One has rose and blue "collar" and other has silver. One has the star metal brads and other is plain. Both are straight-leg walkers. Tag: Guardian Angel. Left: Courtesy Vivian Brady. Right: Courtesy Sandra Crane.

"Guardian Angel", #480-1954. Pink gown with gold trim that is a variation to other pink angels and matches the silver trim gown. White multi-layer wings, gold color harp. Tag: Guardian Angel. Courtesy Jay Minter.

"Guardian Angel", #480-1954. Straight-leg walker. Gown is pale pink with gold trim. Has multi-layer pink dotted Swiss wings. Plastic headpiece halo fits around head and is held on with chin strap. Tag: Guardian Angel. Courtesy Marge Meisinger.

1953-54 "Christening Dress". Straight-leg non-walker. Organdy and cotton lace, long slip that is tagged: Alexander-kin. Molded hair spray-painted yellow blonde. Courtesy Joanna Brunken.

Doll and slip from 1954. The slip is a fine cotton with satin ribbon insert trim and straps. Snaps in back and is tagged: Alexander-kin. The velvet coat is #625-1956. Courtesy Jay Minter.

"Maypole Dance", 1954. Straight-leg walker. Pale blue pastel dress and pale pink pastel apron pinafore. Pink socks and blue shoes. Blue ribbon in hair. Tag: Alexander-kin. Courtesy Bernice Hester.

"Maypole Dance", 1954. Straight-leg walker. Pastel pink organdy dress with pastel blue pinafore that ties in back. Straw hat with flowers and same hat as used on other dolls of this year. Tag: Alexander-kin. Courtesy Linda Crowsey.

"Maypole Dance", 1954. Straight-leg walker but should be on straight-leg non-walker. Variation of color dress and pinafore. Straw hat, shoes and socks are missing. Tag: Alexander-kin. Courtesy Billie McCabe.

Both are "Maypole Dance" of 1954. Straight-leg walker and straight-leg non-walker. Left: Same costume as shown above but has replaced hat and socks. Right: White cotton dress with pink pinafore and hat has been added. Tag: Alexander-kin. Courtesy Joanna Brunken.

"Spring Holiday", 1954. Taffeta coat with two-button closure and a paler pink lining. Sleeveless taffeta dress under coat matches lining. Beautifully styled straw hat with flowers tucked under the brim. Straight-leg walker. Replaced shoes and socks. Tag: Alexander-kin. Courtesy Billie McCabe.

"Shopping With Auntie", #388-1954. Straight-leg walker. The jacket and cap are felt with braid trim and tiny pearl buttons. Replaced socks. Tagged: Alexander-kin. (Author)

"Shopping With Auntie", #388-1954. Shown on a straight-leg non-walker. Replaced socks. Courtesy Sandra Crane.

1954

Front and back view of 1954 sunsuit. Straight-leg walker. Suit wraps between legs and is then tied in the back. Tag: Alexander-kins. (Author).

1954 Sunsuit with rickrack trim and matching bonnet with white bow. Straight-leg non-walker. Original shoes and socks. This style used through the 1960's. Tag: Alexander-kins. Courtesy Billie McCabe.

1953-1954 Straight-leg non-walker in early floral print sunsuit. Replaced shoes and socks. Courtesy Gary Green.

"Rainy Day" set, 1954. Straight-leg non-walker. Vinyl with button opening and matching vinyl bonnet. Boots and purse added. Tag: Alexander-kin. Courtesy Florence Phelps.

"Little Madaline" in the Neiman-Marcus special clothes. Doll has special hairdo. The slacks are attached to a red/white stripped top. Courtesy Lillian Roth.

"Little Madaline", 1954. Straight-leg walker. Made for Neiman-Marcus. All clothes tagged: Alexander-kin, except for white gown with red trim, which looks very much like Alexander quality. The wood case is 9½" x 6" x 6". The "Madaline" doll had a special side part hairdo. Courtesy Christine McWilliams.

1954 ''Bible Children'' and some of the rarest Madame Alexander dolls. The girls all have dark wigs and the boys have red caracul wigs. Upper left: ''Queen Esther.'' Upper right: ''Miriam.'' Lower left: ''Ruth'' and her sheath of wheat. Lower right: ''Rachael.'' Two of these dolls are in color on following pages. Black and white photos are courtesy of Madame Alexander.

1954 "Bible Children". Upper left: "David." Upper right: "Jacob." Lower left: "Joseph." Lower right: "Samuel" who carried a candle as a light to the world. Note girl-style hairdo. Photos courtesy Madame Alexander.

"Ruth" of the 1954 "Bible Children." Courtesy Billie McCabe.

"Rachael" of the 1954 "Bible Children." Courtesy Billie McCabe.

"Joseph" of the 1954 "Bible Children." Courtesy Billie McCabe.

"David" of the 1954 "Bible Children". Courtesy Billie McCabe.

"Juliet" #473 and "Romeo" #474. Both 1955. Straight-leg walkers. She wears a brocade gown and overdress as shown in the United Artists production of "Romeo and Juliet" (1954-55). She has hair in a very special hairdo and he has red caracul wig. Tags: Alexander-kins. Courtesy Roberta Lago.

"Little Godey Lady", #491-1955. Straight-leg walker. Cerise taffeta gown and black felt jacket with black beading. Matching hat with feather plume and rose. Tag: Alexander-kin. Courtesy Roberta Lago.

"Wendy Does The Mambo", #481-1955. Straight-leg walker. Has separate shawl and earrings are sewn to wig. The fan is lace and she wears a rose in her hair. Unusual hairdo and came with full bangs as well as side forehead curls. Courtesy Vivian Brady.

"Wendy Bridesmaid", #478-1955. Straight-leg walker. Nylon tulle over silk organza. Pink flowers and leaves at waist and band of pink flowers with green leaves forming a flower cap. Pink satin tie shoes. Tagged: Alexander-kin. Photo by Richard Olsen of Roosevelt-Baker Photo Co.

"Little Southern Belle Type", 1955. Straight-leg walker. Inset lace in skirt, flowers at waist and blue/pink flowers in bonnet. Replaced shoes. Tag: Alexander-kin. Courtesy Gary Green.

"Wendy Bridesmaid", #478-1955. Straight-leg walker. Same description as previous doll, but has variation of flowers. Tagged: Alexander-kin. Courtesy Lillian Roth.

Close-up of how the headband is formed with the use of flowers and leaves. Courtesy Lillian Roth.

"Wendy Ready For Garden Party", #488-1955. Straight-leg walker. Lace trimmed organza. Flowers tied to wrist and on hat. Inset ribbon on bodice and ribbon streamer tie bow. Pink shoes. There can be variations of flowers used on hat and nosegay, but some flowers on each must match. Tag: Alexander-kin. Courtesy Karen Vincent.

"Queen Elizabeth in Court Gown", #499-1955. Crown has center "leaf" and two silver flower-style pieces on each side. "Diamonds" are in the center of each. She wears a gold bracelet with "diamonds", a "pearl" necklace and gold slip on shoes. Tag: Alexander-kin. Standing beside her is an English Guard. 1966-68. Photo by Richard Olsen of Roosevelt-Baker Photo Co.

"Lady In Waiting", #487-1955. Satin with side panniers of tulle and flowers, coronet and tulle veil. Coronet can also be gold mesh. "Queen", #499-1955. Brocade gown and scarlet velvet robe. Both are straight-leg walkers. Both tagged: Alexander-kin. Courtesy Gene Beckman.

"The Best Man", #461-1955. White dinner jacket and black trousers, maroon tie and cummerbund. Red caracul wig. Straight-leg walker. Tag: Alexander-kin. One pearl button missing from jacket. The 1955 "Groom" is very hard to find and he has a full vest-like white shirt front with no cummerbund and has a bow tie. Courtesy Nancy Celletti.

"Wendy Bride", #475-1955. Straight-leg walker. Another style of "Juliet" cap with satin edging and flowers at the sides. Tag: Alexander-kin. Courtesy Marge Meisinger.

"Wendy Plans Shopping Trip With Grandma", #486-1955. Straight-leg walker. One-piece top and pleated skirt, felt jacket and bonnet. Tag: Alexander-kin. Similar style bonnet as used on #463-1955, but with flowers. Boy is "Bobby, The Boy Next Door", #347-1957. Courtesy Jay Minter.

"Wendy Loves To Waltz", #476-1955. Straight-leg walker. Organdy with red edging and sash. Dress is on doll with bangs, top part of hair pulled back into curls on back of head and rest of hair in regular flip hair style. Has red satin bag attached to wrist. Tagged: Alexander-kin. Courtesy Jay Minter.

"Wendy Does The Highland Fling", #484-1955. The Tartan sash drapes down over the back three-fourths of the way to the hem of the gown. Matching cap with feather plume. There can be a variation of plaid and also of feather plume. Replaced slip. Tag: Alexander-kin. Courtesy Gary Green.

Shows a mint plume on front of cap for "Wendy Does The Highland Fling", #484-1955. Courtesy Vivian Brady.

Wendy's Going With Mother", #418-1955. Straight-leg walker. Organdy dress and matching bonnet with dotted organdy bodice and bonnet insert. Tag: Alexander-kin. Replaced shoes, should have pink ones. Courtesy Jay Minter.

"Wendy Ready For Her Party" with fresh hairdo. #421-1955. Straight-leg walker. Organdy dress and pinafore with tape and lace trim. Doll wears "special hairdo" rolled to back with ribbon. Courtesy Florence Phelps.

"Wendy Helps Mummy Garden", #422-1955. Straight-leg walker. Check dress and plain pinafore with large pocket. She originally came with a tiny garden hoe attached to wrist. There are variations of check material and various colors of both dress and pinafore. Courtesy Jay Minter.

"Wendy Helps Mummy", #428-1955. Straight-leg walker. Candy-striped pinafore over taffeta dress and red shoes and socks. Hair is in ponytails with red ribbons. Tag: Alexander-kin. Courtesy Florence Phelps.

"Wendy Dressed For Summer Morning", #424-1955. Straight-leg walker. Cotton dress with floral pinafore. Has "special hair-do" with ribbon. Came in various colors and floral prints. Tag: Alexander-kin. Courtesy Florence Phelps.

Back view of the "Wendy Dressed For Summer Morning", #424-1955. The hairdo is rolled with side part. Courtesy Florence Phelps.

"Grandma Comes To Tea", #437-1955. Straight-leg walker. Cowl collar with one button (pin accidently left on collar). The organdy of the dress has printed-on (embossed) small flowers. Pink satin sash. Shoes may be replaced. Courtesy Christine McWilliams.

"Wendy Plays in the Garden" #440-1955. Straight-leg walker. Checked dress and matching bonnet, plain pinafore with three pockets. Came with stuffed animal. Courtesy Florence Phelps.

"Wendy's Smart School Outfit", #441-1955. Pique combined with cotton print. Came with white straw hat with red band around brim and streamers. Is shown on bend-knee walker but should be on straight-leg walker. Replaced hat. Courtesy Gary Green.

"Wendy Loves This School Dress", #442-1955. Straight-leg walker. Came in various colors of check and plain for pinafore. Brim of hat should be turned up in a "cup" shape and should have pink shoes. Courtesy Vivian Brady.

Left: "School Dress", #444-1955. Straight-leg walker. Floral print pinafore with ruffle around hem. Straw hat with ribbon on brim and bow. Hair is in pigtails and tied with green ribbon. Right: "Visitors Day At School", #450-1955. Straight-leg walker. Both are tagged: Alexander-kins. Courtesy Gene Beckman.

"School Dress", #444-1955. Straight-leg walker. Has variation of print on pinafore and flower on hat may be replaced. (Author)

"Wendy's Dress for Tea Party at Grandma's", #447-1955. Straight-leg walker. Organdy trimmed with rickrack. White hat with leaves and fruit. Tag: Alexander-kin. Courtesy Linda Crowsey.

"Wendy Helps Cutting Flowers", #448-1955. (Typographical error shows #445 in Vol. 1, page 124). Straight-leg walker. Polished cotton pinafore without shoulder straps and has large pocket, rickrack trim. Toy added. Courtesy Florence Phelps.

"Wendy Walks Her Dog", #456-1955. Straight-leg walker. Check dress with yoke inset of organza. Replaced hat and dog. Courtesy Florence Phelps.

"Visitors Day At School", #450-1955. Straight-leg walker. Polished cotton dress and check pinafore. Straw hat with flowers. Courtesy Pat Timmons.

"Visitors Day At School", #450-1955 showing what the hat looks like when the brim is lowered. The hat is more often found in this position than the original "cup" shape. (Author)

"Wendy" in boxed outfit #0615, which is number on the separate clothing box. 1955. Straight-leg walker. Organdy dress with wide lace collar, applied felt flowers and wears an embroidery-starched lace with metal eyelets on sides for ribbon to go through. This bonnet is identical to one used on "Easter" of 1953-1954 (see that section for doll). It is not known if the hat is original to dress. Courtesy Vivian Brady.

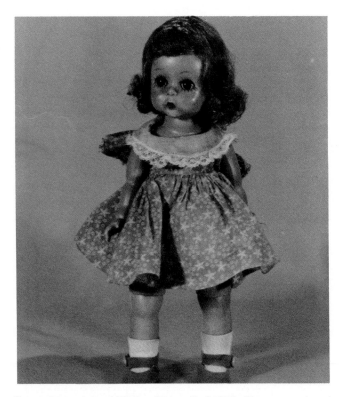

Separate packaged "School Dress" of 1955. Shown on a bend-knee walker but should be on a straight-leg walker. Has large sash that ties in the back. Courtesy Gary Green.

"School Dress" of 1955 shown on straight-leg walker. Original lace bonnet with ribbon trim and ties. Bonnet has ruffle lace trim on front. Tag: Alexander-kin. Courtesy Jay Minter.

"Wendy Goes To Sunday School", #457-1955. Is on a bend-knee doll but should be on a straight-leg walker. Lace-trimmed organdy and starched embroidery and net lace bonnet with flowers on sides. Tag: Alexander-kin. Courtesy Vivian Brady.

"Wendy Calls On Grandma", #459-1955. Shown on bend-knee walker but should be on straight-leg walker. Taffeta dress and dotted Swiss pinafore. Came in several color combinations and also variations to number and kind of flowers on hat. Courtesy Pat Timmons.

"Wendy Visits Auntie", #469-1955. Straight-leg walker. Satin dress with lace trim. Straw hat with nylon net and flower. Tag: Alexander-kin. Courtesy Linda Crowsey.

Separate boxed outfit #0418-1955. Courtesy Marge Meisinger.

These dresses came in many colors and the black floral pinafore was used from 1953 to 1956. The dolls can also come with different color floral print cotton pinafores and the floral pattern can be different. Left: Courtesy Elinor Bibby. Right: Courtesy Pat Timmons.

"Wendy Dressed For Maypole Dance", #458-1955. Straight-leg walker. Taffeta dress with yoke of organza. Has row of lace attached to hem line. The flower circlet on her head is felt, backed with material rosettes, rhinestones and has a pink plastic flower brad holding it together at the back. Circlet is held in place by a chin strap. Tag: Alexander-kin. Courtesy Gene Beckman.

"Wendy Ann Trousseau" of 1955. Packaged by Madame Alexander Doll Company and sold thorugh Marshall-Fields stores in trunk with trousseau of all tagged clothes. Floral print nylon dress. Had plain green straw bonnet. Straight-leg walker and can also be on bend-knee walker as the outfit was separate in 1956 as 0388 and in the company catalog as #0388 "The Prettiest Girl You Know" in 1957. Courtesy Linda Crowsey.

"School Dress", 1955. Straight-leg walker and tagged: Alexander-kin. Cotton dress and fine cotton eyelet pinafore. Bows in hair replaced. Courtesy Jay Minter.

"Wendy Loves Pinafores", #429-1955. Straight-leg walker. Polished cotton dress and strapless pinafore with bow. Hat originally had more flowers around top. Tag: Alexander-kin. Courtesy Pat Timmons.

Variation of "Wendy Loves Pinafores", #429-1955. Straight-leg walker. 1955. Strapless dotted Swiss pinafore with bow over taffeta dress. Soft rayon straw hat has matching bow as on pinafore. Should have pink socks and shoes. Tag: Alexander-kin. (Author).

Yet another variation of "Wendy Loves Pinafores", #429-1955. Straight-leg walker of 1955. Dotted Swiss dress and strapless pinafore with bow attached. Tag: Alexander-kin. Dress is sleeveless with lace trim. Purse added. Should have pink shoes and socks. Courtesy Elinor Bibby.

"Wendy's First Sailor Dress", #576-1955. Cotton with French sailor hat. Also came with red socks and white shoes. Bend-knee walker. Tag: Alexander-kin. Courtesy Doris Richardson.

"Wendy Goes Marketing". Straight-leg walker. Braids with ribbons. Three pink "buttons" on bodice. Replaced shoes. Has sash that ties in back. Tag: Alexander-kin. Courtesy Elinor Bibby.

"Play Dress", 1955. Taffeta with lace on bodice and sleeves. Tag: Alexander-kin. Shown on "Special Hairdo" doll of 1955 which is a straight-leg walker. Courtesy Jay Minter.

Robe from 1954 to 1958. Leatherette slippers with pompons. Bend-knee walker. Tag: Alexander-kin or Madame Alexander, etc. Courtesy Pat Timmons.

"Baby Clown", #464-1955. Straight-leg walker. Same description as clown below, but has different color combination to clown suit and medium cheek color. Courtesy Vivian Brady.

"Baby Clown", #464-1955. Straight-leg walker. Two-tone suit. Separate neck ruff that ties in back. Painted face, bright red caracul wig. Extremely pale cheek color. Gold boots. Small pipe cleaner dog named "Huggy". Courtesy Bernice Heister.

"Baby Clown" has same description as other ones, but has deep cheek color. The other clown is "Pierrot" of 1956. See that section of this book for full description. Courtesy Gary Green.

"Wendy In Dude Ranch Outfit", #570-1956 and brother "Bill", #373B-1957. Her boots match the color of her jeans and the straw hat is rolled at sides and tied. He is wearing same outfit as "Wendy" #571-1956. Boy's hairdo. Cart and harness made by Ken Beckman. Courtesy Gene Beckman.

"Davy Crockett Boy and Girl", 1955. Straight-leg walkers. He has red caracul wig and she a red flip hairdo wig. Suedine material clothes, leatherette fringe, boots, belt with metal buckle and metal brads over closures of jackets. Skirt is attached to plain top on the girl. Plush "Coonskin" caps. Girl has gun added. Courtesy Margaret Mándel.

"Wendy Is Good At Tennis", #415-1955. Straight-leg walker. Cotton twill shorts with two buttons and cotton knit bodysuit and tie shoes. Wears glasses and has tennis racket tied to wrist, which can come in various colors. Tag: Alexander-kin. Courtesy Margaret Mandel.

"Wendy Visits A Dude Ranch", #449-1955. One-piece bodysuit with long sleeves and one button in front. Denim jeans with metal brads at the sides of the leg, boots and straw sombrero-style hat with decorations. Courtesy Bernice Heister.

"Wendy Visits A Dude Ranch", #449-1955. Same description as other doll, but has different plaid body suit. Straight-leg walker. Tagged: Alexander-kins. Courtesy Lillian Roth.

"Wendy In Her Drum Majorette Costume", #482-1955. Straight-leg walker. Rayon taffeta body with rose and gold trim, matching separate skirt. Green felt vest trimmed with gold braid and gold boots. The hat is taffeta with gold braid and feather plumes. Replaced baton. Courtesy Margaret Mandel.

"Wendy In Her Majorette Costume", #482-1955. Straight-leg walker. One-piece bodysuit with long sleeves and matching skirt. Has vest that is felt trimmed with gold braid. Taffeta hat with gold braid and gold metal piece on side that matches the top of baton. Green feather plume. Photo by Richard Olsen of Roosevelt-Baker Photo Co.

"Baby Angel", #480-1955. Straight-leg walker. Nylon tulle, satin and multi-layer material wings, which can be white or pink. Silver or gold tie shoes. The catalog for 1955 shows the same halo style as used on the 1954 "Angel", except the 1955 version has small flowers around the edge, but there are too many of this style halo in collections for it to not be correct. Plastic ring held on by covered wire sewn to back of gown. Courtesy Jay Minter.

"Baby Angel", #480-1955. Straight-leg walker. Satin and tulle gown with row of lace around sleeves. Multi-layer chiffon wings that have a soft dotted Swiss layer on back side. Clear plastic ring with silver paper around outside edge makes the halo. Silver harp. Both harp and halo have pink felt flowers. Tag: Alexander-kin. Courtesy Jan Cravens.

"Wendy Goes Roller Skating", #426-1955. Straight-leg walker. This outfit came boxed as #0426 in 1955. Different color bodysuit and has beanie with berries. This same beany can come with a feather in place of the berries. Tag: Alexander-kins. Courtesy Marge Meisinger.

"Wendy Goes Roller Skating", #426-1955. Straight-leg walker but is shown on a bend-knee walker. Jersey bodysuit with taffeta skirt and shoe skates. Missing is beany cap with feather or berries. Courtesy Linda Crowsey.

"Wendy Loves Her Ballet Lessons", #454-1955. Straight-leg walker. One-piece satin tutu with skirt of nylon tulle. Has circlet in hair made of plastic with three plastic roses. Courtesy Florence Phelps.

"Wendy Loves Her Ballet Lessons", #454-1955. Straight-leg walker with satin and nylon tulle tutu. Plastic flowers in hair. Has "Juliet" hairdo. A few of the 1956 ballerinas also had this same hair style and were made due to the need to use up the excess dolls with this hair style. Courtesy Lillian Roth.

"Wendy Goes to Rodeo", #484-1955. Straight-leg walker. Same description as doll below, but has variation of braid used on edge of sombrero-style hat. Courtesy Shirley Kronkowski.

Side view of "Wendy Goes To Rodeo" to show variation of braid used at edge of sombrero hat and also the design used on the green boots. Courtesy Shirley Kronkowski.

"Wendy Goes To Rodeo", #484-1955. Straight-leg walker. Suede cloth outfit trimmed with fringe and felt. Hair is in braids with green ribbons and has green boots with gold painted design. Tag: Alexander-kins. Courtesy Lillian Roth.

"Wendy's School Coat", #451-1955. Straight-leg walker. Under coat is plain pique dress. Outfit came with a red or a white hat with red trim. Tag: Alexander-kin. Courtesy Florence Phelps.

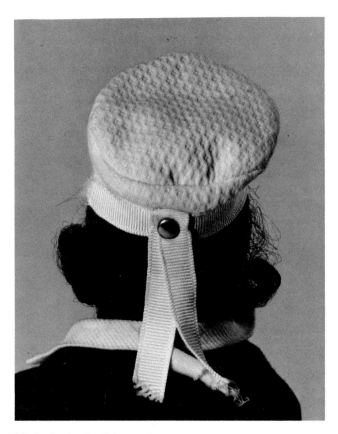

"Wendy Ready For A Stroll In the Park", #438-1955. Straight-leg walker. Plain taffeta dress with lace trim and gabardine coat with white collars and cuffs of waffle pique. Matching pique hat. Tag: Alexander-kin. Shown in Vol. 1 as #464 and should be #438. Courtesy Gloria Harris.

This is the back of the waffle pique hat for the outfit "Wendy Ready For A Stroll In The Park", #438-1955. Courtesy Gloria Harris.

"Wendy Dressed For Matinee", #0456. Matches with 18" "Binnie Walker" #1856-1955 "Dressed For Matinee". Has tatting lace around collar. Straight-leg walker. Courtesy Jay Minter.

"Wendy Changes Outfits For Rainy Day", #439-1955. Straight-leg walker. Tag: Alexander-kin. Shown in Vol. 1 as #449, and should be 439. Courtesy Linda Crowsey.

"Wendy Likes A Rainy Day", #453-1955. Straight-leg walker. Coat and bonnet came in several color variations. Some were polka-dot with solid linings, others were solid colors with polka-dot linings. All linings matched the dress under the coat. This style used 1953 to 1959. Courtesy Vivian Brady.

Left: "Wendy Ready For Any Weather", #572-1956. Rayon taffeta coat lined to match her floral print dress. Yellow rayon socks and brown boots. Matching rain bonnet with brim turned up. Right: "Wendy Goes To Matinee", 1955-1956 #463. Bend-knee walker. Gabardine coat with wide collar, white felt hat with flowers and can also have feather plume. Tag: Alexander-kin. Courtesy Margaret Mandel.

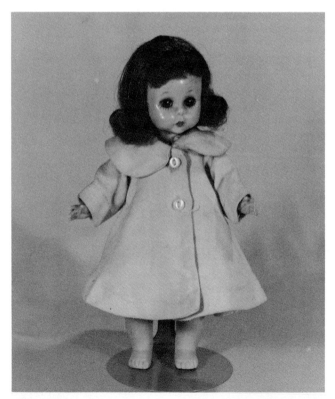

"Wendy Goes To The Matinee", #463-1955. Straight-leg walker. Variation of color used for coat, missing bonnet, shoes and socks. Used as boxed outfit #0595-1956 with flowers on hat. Courtesy Gary Green.

"Wendy Likes A Rainy Day", #453-1955. Straight-leg walker. Doll is all original including the blue boots and unusual longer socks. Tag: Alexander-kins. Courtesy Marge Meisinger.

Matching vinyl rain coat and hat with blue trim. The larger doll is 18″ size in extra boxed outfit #411-1954-1955. This outfit came in 15″, 18″ and 25″ sizes. The 8″ "Wendy Ann" is in boxed outfit #0453-1955. This same rain set came in polka-dots with plain cuffs and collar edges. Courtesy Gary Green.

"Wendy Goes Visiting", #462-1955. Straight-leg walker. Felt jacket over polished cotton dress with pleated skirt. Matching bonnet with pompon. Brim of hat should be standing up. Courtesy Billie McCabe.

"Wendy Loves Her Cardigan", #467-1955. Straight-leg walker. Pleated skirt dress with wool jersey cardigan and pixie hat. The cardigan is trimmed with flower appliques around sleeves and neck. Courtesy Florence Phelps.

"Wendy Goes On Train Journey", #468-1955. Straight-leg walker. Pleated skirt with plain white top and white felt jacket with metal stars on closures and sleeves. Hat may be a replacement. Outfit in catalog shows a beany, but variations can be found. Courtesy Billie McCabe.

"Wendy Ready For Plane Trip", #452-1955. Straight-leg walker. Variation of pleated skirt to cotton dress (attached plain top). Tag: Alexander-kins, and also comes with tag: Madame Alexander, etc. Courtesy Florence Phelps.

"Wendy Ready For Plane Trip", #452-1955. Straight-leg walker. Plain sleeveless dress with pleated skirt, felt jacket with metal "buttons". Matching beany with pompons. Courtesy Pat Timmons.

"Wendy's Train Journey", #468-1955. Shown on a bend-knee walker but doll should be a straight-leg walker. Plaid dress with pleated skirt, felt jacket with buttons and beanie cap with pompons. Tag: Alexander-kins. Photo by Richard Olsen of Roosevelt-Baker Photo Co.

"Wendy's Train Journey", #468-1955. Straight-leg walker. Variation of plaid used on dress with pleated skirt, white felt jacket with buttons, matching beanie with pompons. Right: "Wendy Dressed For A Summer Day", #432-1959. Bend-knee walker. One-piece outfit and matching panties. Replaced beanie. Tag: Alexander-kin. Courtesy Margaret Mandel.

"Wendy Loves To Swim", #406-1955. Straight-leg walker. Lace trimmed taffeta, net beach hat, sandals and glasses. Tag: Alexander-kin. Courtesy Florence Phelps.

"Wendy On Way To Beach", #427-1955. Straight-leg walker. Cotton suit and coat. The 1956 set has a cotton suit but a pique coat. The beach bag is felt with a design on front. This outfit came in various colors. Glasses are missing. Tag: Alexander-kins. Courtesy Vivian Brady.

Variations in color of Beach outfit of 1955. All are straight-leg walkers. Left: shoes/socks replaced, beach bag added and hat missing. Center: Replaced shoes and beach hat, glasses missing. Right: Beach towel added. Courtesy Gary Green.

1955 Sunsuit with rows of lace at the bottom and has matching bonnet. Socks are replaced and tied oxford shoes may be replaced. Courtesy Elinor Bibby.

"Wendy Plays On Beach", #403-1955. Straight-leg walker. Denim playsuit and metal shovel attached to wrist. Replaced shoes. Should be white side snap shoes with no socks. Cap added. Tag: Alexander-kin. Courtesy Florence Phelps.

Pajamas are #0425-1955-1957. Came in many different prints and checks. Tagged: Alexander-kin. The robe is from 1955 and 1956 and came in various colors and prints. The robe came with both matching pajamas and plain color sleeveless gown with open lacework, and threaded ribbon through it around the waist. Tagged: Alexander-kin. Courtesy Gary Green.

"Wendy At Bedtime" set of 1955-1957. Came in various color combinations and prints. Suedine slippers with pompons. Tagged: Alexander-kin. Courtesy Bernice Heister.

Floral sleeping gown is from 1953-1955. Straight-leg non-walker or can be on straight-leg walker or bend-knee walker. Had red slippers with white pompons and pink bow at waist. Tag: Alexander-kin. Courtesy Vivian Brady.

The white gown is #0401-1955 with ribbon threaded through lace at waist and the robe is a variation of #0425-1955. Straight-leg walker. Tagged: Alexander-kin. Courtesy of and childhood doll of Cathy Ruggiero.

Variation of material and use of rickrack on the 1953 to 1956 pajamas that were boxed separately. The boy is "Bill" #320-1960. Courtesy Roberta Lago.

This set of cotton pajamas can be on a straight-leg non-walker, straight-leg walker or bend-knee walker as they were sold separately for several years. The material can differ as well as the color. Tagged: Alexander-kins. Courtesy Loramay Wilson.

Ca. 1955-1968. Floral and dotted nylon with crepe robe. There can be a snap at neck or robe can come with streamers to tie. The leatherette slippers for these robes and gowns have a pompon on top. Courtesy Pat Timmons.

"Neiman-Marcus" special doll dress of 1955. Straight-leg walker. Name of store printed on material. Came in case and doll also sold separately, as was the dress. The dress is tagged: Jane Miller/Lafayette, Calif. and is an excellent quality outfit. The other two dresses are poor quality and not tagged. The tiny suitcase is marked: "Samsonite" and there are glasses, magazines, extra socks and small wire hangers. Came in red and white case. Doll's hairdo is #424-1955. Courtesy Christine McWilliams.

"Neiman-Marcus" dress could come on a special hairdo (#424-1955) or regular hairdo doll, in 1955 and these dolls were straight-leg walkers. The dress was sold separately and can be on a bend-knee walker also. Courtesy Elinor Bibby.

Toddler "Little Genius" straight-leg walker. 1955 and pre-dating the bent limb baby of 1956. Full bodysuit of cotton knit with angora trim at neck and sleeves. Tagged: Little Genius. Highly colored, no bottom lashes and rug-type wig. "Bill" is a bent-knee walker sold as a basic doll. Shorts tagged: Alexander-kin. Original tie shoes. Boxing gloves and football added. Courtesy Margaret Mandel.

1955 sold through FAO Schwarz. Box is regular Alexander designed with pink inside and box is blue covered with pink flowers. Box is 10½" x 12½". The "Wendy Ann" is a straight-leg walker and her dress is tagged: Alexander-kin. All clothes in the box are tagged: Alexander-kin. Courtesy Lahunta McIntyre.

"Southern Belles", 1956. Bend-knee walkers and tagged: Alexander-kin. Pink: Has magenta shoes, double strand white crystal necklace, purple straw hat with purple veil over eyes and veil extends around to the back of the hat. Blonde flip hairdo with curls under hat. Blue: Black shoes, black straw hat trimmed in fruit and flowers. Black loop earrings studded with "diamonds" and wears a special hairdo that is upswept with curls on each side of face and across forehead. Photos by Richard Olsen of Roosevelt-Baker Photo Co.

Back view of the "Southern Belle" outfit for 1956.

Back of blue "Southern Belle" of 1956. Note how hair is parted in back.

"Wendy Goes To Ballet", #601-1956. Bend-knee walker. Soft taffeta with yoke of velvet. Missing is frilly tulle bandeau on head. Should have tie shoes. Tag: Alexander-kin. Courtesy Sharon Griffiths.

"Flowergirl", #602-1956. Bend-knee walker. Satin gown with double loop beaded "buckle" holding sash. Pink tie shoes. Flowers in pulled-back hairdo. Tag: Alexander-kin. Courtesy Pat Timmons.

"Wendy Dressed For June Wedding", #605-1956. Bend-knee walker. Taffeta gown and flower trimmed hat. Should have gold slippers. Tag: Alexander-kin. Courtesy Sandra Crane.

"Wendy's First Long Dancing Dress", #606-1956. Bend-knee walker. Tag: Alexander-kin. Side part hairdo has rolled curl and curls in back tied with ribbon matching sash, as well as a plastic flower. Courtesy Marge Meisinger.

"Wendy's First Long Dancing Dress", #606-1956. Bend-knee walker. Nylon tulle gown, velvet sash and ribbon in back of hairdo with ribbon being glued down in the middle under the curls. Tag: Alexander-kin. (Author)

"Wendy Goes To Garden Party", #620-1956. Bend knee walker. Swiss organdy gown. Straw hat with flowers and streamers. Back view shows hat and streamers. Tag: Alexander-kin. Courtesy Shirley Kronkowski.

"Wendy Dressed In Ballgown", #623-1956. Bend-knee walker. Taffeta gown trimmed with roses, gold tiara with "diamonds". Gold shoes. Tag: Alexander-kin. Photo by Richard Olsen of Roosevelt-Baker Photo Co.

"Story Princess", #892-1956. Nylon tulle with rose underslip lined in white. Bend-knee walker. Matches the larger "Cissy"-faced "Story Princess" that was available in 15″ and 18″ size. From the television show "Howdy Doody". Photo by Richard Olsen of Roosevelt-Baker Photo Co.

"Bridesmaid", #621-1956. Bend-knee walker. Taffeta gown with roses, pink sash and bandeau with flowers on each side. Gold shoes. Courtesy Gary Green.

"Cousin Karen", #630-1956. Bend-knee walker. Floral cotton gown with velvet bodice and purse. Straw hat with flowers. White snap shoes. Tag: Alexander-kin. Courtesy Lillian Roth.

"Melanie", #633-1956. Bend-knee walker. Velvet gown with hat and parasol of tulle. Pink roses on hat and parasol. Tulle slip, necklace and jewel on bodice. Hair pulled to back of head. Courtesy Gene Beckman.

"Wendy Flowergirl", #543-1956. Bend-knee walker. Matches with "Baby Genius" #756-1956. Is missing lacy bonnet and basket of pink and lavender flowers. Courtesy Linda Crowsey.

"Wendy Comes To Breakfast", #537-1956. Bend-knee walker. Dotted Swiss dress with lace trim and attached to underneath hem. Hairdo is correct to dress, but had small flower at the one side. Ribbon added. Should have white shoes. Tag: Alexanderkin. Courtesy Margaret Mandel.

"Wendy's Perky Hairdo", #539-1956. Bend-knee walker. Floral print pique dress with ribbon trim and rickrack at neck and sleeves. Tag: Alexander-kin. Courtesy Doris Richardson.

"Wendy Invites Guest For Luncheon", #542-1956. Organdy dress came in many pastel shades. Should be on bend-knee walker but is shown on a straight-leg walker and straight-leg non-walker. Hair bow is missing. Tag: Alexander-kin. Courtesy Gary Green.

"Wendy Invites Guest For Luncheon", #542-1956. Bend-knee walker. Original hair bow. Came in various shades of pastels. Tag: Alexander-kin. Courtesy Vivian Brady.

"Wendy Goes To Sunday School", #587-1956. Bend-knee walker. Taffeta dress with lace trim on dress and straw hat and has satin sash. Tag: Alexander-kin. Courtesy Jay Minter.

"Wendy At Home", #544-1956. Taffeta dress with lace attached to hem underneath. Came on bend-knee walker doll with hair-do pulled back at the top, full bangs, and tied with ribbon. Also came as extra boxed outfit. (Author)

Lower left: ''Wendy School Dress'' boxed dress of 1964-1965. Hairdo is from 1965. Slip added. Bend-knee walker. Center: ''Wendy At Home'', #544-1956. Bend-knee walker. Tag: Alexander-kin. Ribbon added to hairdo. Lower right: ''Wendy After School'' dress which came in various colors and trim styles. Mostly sold as extra boxed outfit. 1956. Bend-knee walker and tagged: Alexander-kin. Courtesy Margaret Mandel.

Lower left: "Wendy Carries Her Milk Money", #553-1956. One-piece bodysuit of cotton with striped pinafore buttoned to bodysuit, straw hat with red trim. Carries plastic purse. Center: "Wendy Off To See Grandma", #573-1956. Polished cotton, organdy pinafore with lace trim, straw hat with looped ribbon bow. Right: "Wendy At Sunday Breakfast", #536-1956. Taffeta dress, lace trim and embroidered trim of pink flowers and leaves at waist. White felt hat with flowers should go with #531-1958. All are bend-knee walkers and clothes are tagged: Alexander-kin. Courtesy Margaret Mandel.

Left: "Wendy In Favorite Summer Afternoon Outfit", #584-1956. Bend-knee walker. Organdy dress and pinafore with lace trim. Pink socks and straw hat with flowers. Tag: Alexanderkin. Right: "Wendy Off On Shopping Jaunt", #595-1956. Bend-knee walker. Pin dot cotton dress, organdy pinafore and lace trim. Cute straw hat with flowers. Tag: Alexander-kin. Courtesy Gene Beckman.

"Wendy On A Hot Morning", #585-1956. Bend-knee walker. Tag: Alexander-kin. Replaced straw hat. The hat shown in catalog is of this style but has flowers around top. Courtesy Linda Crowsey.

"Wendy Goes Calling With Mother", #586-1956. Organdy and lace dress and matching straw hat. This dress is often found on the "First Communion" doll of 1957. It is not certain whether or not both dresses were used. Courtesy Bernice Heister.

"Wendy Attending A House Party", #582-1956. Bend-knee walker. Polished cotton dress and taffeta pinafore. The basket of flowers is called a handbag in the 1956 catalog. Replaced straw hat. The original hat is straw with flowers that match the ones in the basket. Tag: Alexander-kin. Courtesy Pat Timmons.

May be variation or boxed set of #483-1956 as the flowers on the waist match the ones on the hat which is pink straw. Bend-knee walker. Courtesy Christine McWilliams.

"Wendy Has Fun Wearing Black Taffeta Pinafore", #583-1956. Bend-knee walker. Organdy dress, straw hat with flowers that match flowers at waist of pinafore. Tag: Alexander-kin. Courtesy Shirley Bertrand.

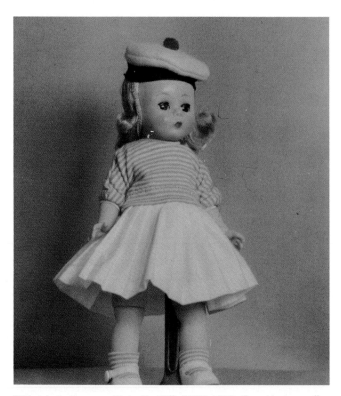

"Wendy In Basque-Style Outfit", #574-1956. Bend-knee walker. One-piece dress with pleated skirt and striped shirt, felt French sailor hat. Striped socks. Tag: Alexander-kin. Courtesy Bernice Heister.

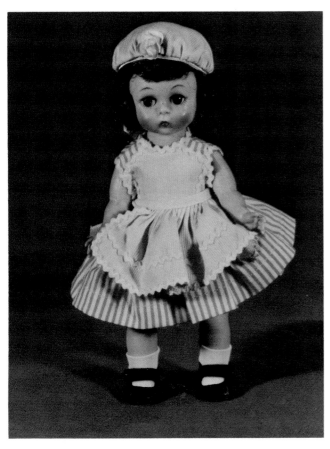

"Wendy Runs To Market", #568-1956. Bend-knee walker. Boxed outfit is #0568. Striped cotton with attached pique pinafore apron and rickrack trim. Replaced shoes, which should be white. Rose on beret. Tag: Alexander-kin. Courtesy Marge Meisinger.

Variation of bonnet on "Wendy Runs To Market", #568-1956. Bend-knee walker. Bonnet of same material as dress and has lace trim. Tag: Alexander-kin. Courtesy Linda Crowsey.

"Wendy Goes Walking", #581-1956. Cotton dress and pinafore with lace trim. Straw bonnet. Came with basket. Right: "Wendy Helps Mummy", #428-1955. Dress is navy taffeta. Both are bend-knee walkers. Tag: Alexander-kin. Courtesy Roberta Lago.

"Wendy Takes Fruit To Grandma", #566-1956. Bend-knee walker. Floral print cotton dress with polished cotton pinafore. Straw basket of fruit. Replaced shoulder strap. The rolled hair-do is correct to doll and the back of the hair was orginally pulled back tightly into "bun". Tag: Alexander-kin. Courtesy Linda Crowsey.

"Wendy Visiting Her Cousins", #559-1956. Bend-knee walker. Braid trimmed pique dress. Tag: Alexander-kin. Courtesy Billie McCabe.

"Wendy Wears Another Polished Cotton Dress", #589-1956. Bend-knee walker. Sleeves and roll collar of rosebud print. The straw hat is unique and has fantastic design. Tag: Alexander-kin. Courtesy Florence Phelps.

Back view of hat for #589-1956. Straw hat has bow and flowers. Courtesy Florence Phelps.

Left: Variation of #592-1956. Bend-knee walker. Replaced shoes and socks. Tag: Alexander-kin. Center: "Wendy Wears Another Simple Dress", #565-1956. Replaced straw hat. Left: "Wendy Goes To School", #460-1955. Replaced shoes and socks and missing hat. Bend-knee walker, but doll should be straight-leg walker. Courtesy Roberta Lago.

Left: "Wendy Calls On School Friend", #594-1956. Bend-knee walker. Striped organdy, satin sash and straw hat with flowers. Tag: Alexander-kin. Right: "Wendy Dressed For Trip To Market With Mommy" #382-1957. Bend-knee walker. Lace edged pinafore over taffeta dress. Straw hat with flowers and ribbon. Tag: Alexander-kin. Courtesy Gene Beckman.

Left: Variation of "Wendy Looks As Sweet As A Lollipop", #326-1957 which came with a felt bonnet with flowers on top. Center: "Wendy Does Homework", 1955, straight-leg walker, replaced shoes and socks. Right: Variation of #518-1956. Bend-knee walker. Replaced shoes and socks. Courtesy Gary Green.

Variation of #518-1956. Bend-knee walker. Came in many different colors and prints. Courtesy Loramay Wilson.

''Wendy After School'', Box #559-1956. Bend-knee walker. Came in various colors. Tag: Alexander-kin. Courtesy Linda Crowsey.

''Wendy After School'', extra boxed outfit #559-1956. Bend-knee walker. Came in various colors. Tag: Alexander-kin. Courtesy Linda Crowsey.

Variation of outfit #559-1956. Bend-knee walker. Tag: Alexander-kin. Courtesy Linda Crowsey.

"Wendy In School Dress", #557-1956. Bend-knee walker. Printed cotton and braid trimmed. Hat may be replaced. Dress came with and without the bow on bodice. The hat goes with outfit #444-1955, "Wendy School Outfit", or it may have come separately, or with this outfit. Courtesy Vivian Brady.

"Interesting Dress from Wendy's Wardrobe", #518-1956. Bend-knee walker. This dress, as others with rickrack trim were basic dresses and were sold in an array of prints and colors and variations. Many were boxed and sold separately and are referred to by Madame Alexander as "Homework Dresses". Courtesy Pat Timmons.

"Bridegroom", #577-1956. Bend-knee walkers. Striped trousers and grey cravats. Left: 1956 and right: #377-1957. Courtesy Gary Green.

"Bridegroom", #577-1956. Bend-knee walker. Striped trousers and grey cravat. Red caracul wig. Courtesy Christine McWilliams.

"Wendy In Bridal Gown", #615-1956. Bend-knee walker. Nylon tulle with matching veil. Part of flowers are missing from headpiece. Tag: Alexander-kin. Courtesy Kathy Bookstein.

"Wendy On School Trip", #569-1956. Bend-knee walker. Plaid dress and matching panties. Corded cotton or pique coat and tam, trimmed with plaid covered buttons. Replaced shoes. Tag: Alexander-kin. Courtesy Sharon Griffiths.

Left: "Wendy On School Trip", #569-1956 to show neckline and sleeves. Right: Dress under coat of "Wendy Dressed In Oriental Influence", #591-1956. Both are bend-knee walkers and both tagged: Alexander-kin. The tufted green chairs are Alexander, covered in velvet with gold braid. 4¾" tall x 4" wide on metal legs. Has gold and black paper label: by Madame Alexander New York. The 2½" wide felt round puff pillows are cut with pinking shears. These pillows also came in floral print. Two chairs slide together to make a couch. From the "Start-A-Home For Alexander-kins" collection of 1956. Courtesy Elizabeth Montsano of Yesterday's Children.

"Parlour Maid", #579-1956. Taffeta dress and organdy apron. "Doily" style headpiece. Bend-knee walker. Tag: Alexander-kin. Courtesy Gloria Harris.

"Parlour Maid", #579-1956. Bend-knee walker. Has replaced dust mop. Variation of trim. Courtesy Lillian Roth.

"Doily"-style headpiece on the #579-1956 "Parlour Maid". Courtesy Vivian Brady.

"Parlour Maid", #579-1956. Bend-knee walker. Replaced dust mop and variation of trim. Tag: Alexander-kin. Courtesy Vivian Brady.

1956

Left: Has "Juliet" hair style and dates from 1956. Bend-knee walker. Center: #364-1957 "Start The Music For Wendy". Right: #564-1955 and also came in Trousseau in an Alexander "window" box in 1956. All are bend-knee walkers and all are tagged: Alexanderkins. Courtesy Florence Phelps.

"Wendy Plays Tennis", #527-1956. Bend-knee walker. Gabardine shorts with striped top. Tie shoes and has plastic tennis racket tied to arm. Glasses missing. Tag: Alexander-kin. Courtesy Florence Phelps.

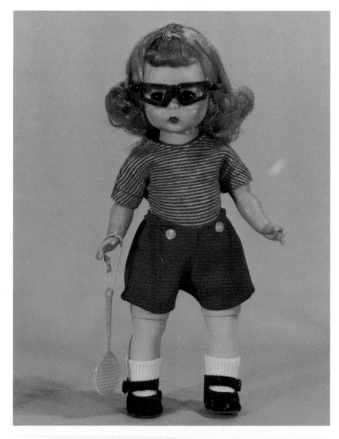

"Wendy Plays Tennis", #527-1956. Bend-knee walker. Gabardine shorts and striped top. Glasses and tennis racket made of plastic. Should have tie shoes. Tag: Alexander-kin. Courtesy Gary Green.

"Wendy Goes Ice Skating", #555-1956. Bend-knee walkers. One-piece bodysuit with felt skirt and felt bonnet. Rickrack trim. Shoe skates. Came in various colors. Tag: Alexander-kin. Courtesy Gary Green.

"Wendy Goes Ice Skating", #555-1956. There can be a variation as to size and location of the rickrack as well as the color of the outfit. Tag: Alexander-kin. Courtesy Gene Beckman.

"Wendy Thinks Roller Skating Is Fun", #556-1956. Bend-knee walker. Felt jumper and short sleeve bodysuit. Pixie-style hat. Felt flowers on skirt and cap. Tag: Alexander-kin. Courtesy Marge Meisinger.

"Wendy Thinks Roller Skating Is Fun", #556-1956. Bend-knee walker. Felt jumper over short sleeve bodysuit. Pixie-style cap. Replaced socks. Felt applied flowers on skirt and cap. Tag: Alexander-kin. Courtesy Jay Minter.

"Wendy Rides Well", #571-1956. Bend-knee walker. Corduroy breeches and white shirt. Leatherette belt and wooden/leatherette riding crop. Matching riding hat with visor. Boots. Tag: Alexander-kin. Courtesy Vivian Brady.

"Wendy Nurse", #563-1956 to 1961. White cotton uniform and cap. Tie shoes. Bend-knee walker. Tag: Alexander-kin. Courtesy Vivian Brady.

"Pierrot", #561-156. Bend-knee walker. Satin outfit and hat with pompons. Satin ribbon tie shoes. Yellow-blonde caracul wig. Dark brown "reindeer". Tag: Alexander-kin. Courtesy Lillian Roth.

"Pierrot", #561-1956. Bend-knee walker. Suit and hat are satin and he has pompons on suit and hat. Satin ribbon shoe ties and has "reindeer" on gold leash. Neck ruff is tulle. The "reindeer" usually is dark brown. Can also have a dog. Caracul wig is yellow-blonde. Tag: Alexander-kin. Courtesy Sandra Crane.

"Wendy On Way To Beach", #541-1956. Bend-knee walker. Pique coat and hat and cotton swimsuit. Glasses and sandals. Had "V" shaped beach bag. Tag: Alexander-kin. Courtesy Bernice Heister.

Lower left: Bend-knee walker. Outfit sold separately. Dotted cotton playsuit, lace trimmed, snap closure at shoulder, elastic waistband in back. Center: Straight-leg walker in boxed nightie and tagged: Alexander-kin. Lower right: Straight-leg walker shown in boxed pajamas of floral crinkle cotton. Sold as boxed outfit. This same material was used for swimsuit #541-1956. Courtesy Margaret Mandel.

Sleep set ca. 1955-1958. Bend-knee walker. Dotted nylon robe that snaps at neck. The dolls are found with both cotton and crepe gowns. Tag: Alexander-kin. Courtesy Billie McCabe.

Shows dress and lining under #572-1956 "Wendy Ready For Any Weather". Brim of rain bonnet turned back. Courtesy Vivian Brady.

"Wendy Needs More Than One Coat", #580-1956. Bend-knee walker. Taffeta dress that matches the lining of gabardine coat and hat. Replaced shoes which should be black. Tag: Alexander-kin. Courtesy Marge Meisinger.

"Wendy Dressed In Oriental Influence", #591-1956. Bend-knee walker. Mandarin coat lined to match dress and Mandarin straw hat. Tag: Alexander-kin. Courtesy Florence Phelps.

Rayon taffeta rain set sold as extra boxed set in 1956. Rain bonnet has gold braid trim. Courtesy Marge Meisinger.

"Wendy Wears A Charming Ensemble", #625-1956. Bend-knee walker. Velvet coat and hat over taffeta dress with velvet ribbon trim. This outfit came in various colors of ribbon trim, coat and hat. Muff with flowers. Replaced shoes which should be white. Coat has taffeta lining same as dress. Tag: Alexander-kin. Courtesy Marge Meisinger.

"Wendy Dressed For Spectator Sports", #578-1956. Bend-knee walker. One-piece dress with pleated skirt, felt jacket and beany with red trim, metal buttons and eagle. Tag: Alexander-kin. Courtesy Florence Phelps.

"Wendy Adores A Cardigan Outfit", #575-1956. Bend-knee walker. One-piece cotton pique dress with pleated skirt and wool jersey cardigan and matching hood. Tag: Alexander-kin. (Author).

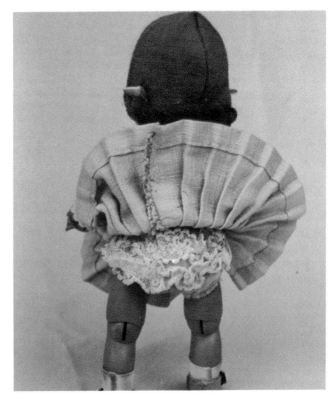

"Wendy Adores A Cardigan", #575-1956. Bend-knee walker. Wool jersey cardigan and hood, one-piece dress with pleated skirt. Variation of colors. Wears very lacy panties. Tags: Alexander-kin. Courtesy Florence Phelps.

"Wendy Travel Trunk", 1956. An exclusive for FAO Schwarz. Has window side for doll and other side for hats and hanging extra clothes. This same case also came with one side having four compartments for clothes. Courtesy Jay Minter.

"Wendy In Case" 1956 for F.A.O. Schwarz. Patent case with "window" door for doll and clothes. Clothes tagged: Alexander-kin. This same case also came as a double width with doll on one side and clothes on other. Courtesy Marge Meisinger.

Left: "Flower Girl #398 and #0398-1957. Bend-knee walker. Wide lace trim and satin ribbon, bows and sash. Missing is bandeau with rows of lace. Tag: Alexander-kin. Right: #470-1963 "Bride". Bend-knee walker. Tag: Alexander-kin. Courtesy Marge Meisinger.

"Cousin Grace", #432-1957. Bend-knee walker. Beautiful lace trimmed gown. Has black ribbon with jewel at neck. Blue shoes and dress ties with wide sash in back. Tag: Alexander-kin. Photo by Richard Olson of Roosevelt-Baker Photo Co.

"Cousin Grace", #432-1957. Variation of material used for gown. Has back ribbon and jewel at neck. Bend-knee walker. Dress ties with wide sash in back. Tag: Alexander-kin. Courtesy Gary Green.

"Nana, Wendy's Governess", #433-1957. Bend-knee walker. Stripe cotton shirt with tiny bead "buttons" on bodice, plain collar and cuffs. Carries round beaded purse (reticule) attached with black chain to wrist. Tag: Alexander-kin and can be tagged: Madame Alexander, etc. Courtesy Florence Phelps.

"Aunt Pitty-Pat", #435-1957. Bend-knee walker. Checked and plain taffeta. Jeweled earrings. Nylon tulle parasol, straw hat with flowers and net. Tag: Alexander-kin. Courtesy Gene Beckman.

"Wendy Graduation", #399-1957. Bend-knee walker. Swiss dotted organdy with blue satin ribbon sash. Has rolled paper attached to wrist. Tag: Alexander-kin. Diploma states: "Wendy has successfully completed her schooling at this institution. William Doll P.H.O. Principal-Madame Alexander School For Dolls." Courtesy Marge Meisinger.

"Wendy In Velvet Party Dress", #389-1957. Bend-knee walker. Velvet jumper with matching bonnet with ribbon. Tag: Alexander-kin. Courtesy Christine McWilliams.

Left: "Aunt Pitty-Pat", #435-1957. Bend-knee walker. Taffeta gown, nylon tulle parasol and straw/net hat with flowers. Tag: Alexander-kin. Right: "Aunt Agatha", #434-1957. Bend-knee walker. Check taffeta gown, black jacket and hat with feathers and net. Carries black purse (reticule). Bend-knee walker. Tag: Alexander-kin. Courtesy Lillian Roth.

"Wendy In Party Sun Dress", #344-1957. Bend-knee walkers. Gold designs on outfits and gold tie slippers. Red outfit is a variation and has a replaced hat and shoes with socks added. Tags: Alexander-kins. Courtesy Gene Beckman.

"Wendy In Play Dress", #346-1957. Bend-knee walker. Cotton dress trimmed with Venetian lace and white-edged bonnet. Tag: Alexander-kin. Courtesy Pat Timmons.

"Wendy Loves School Dresses", #348-1957. Bend-knee walker. Cotton dress with cotton pinafore with ruffle. Missing is black straw hat with yellow flowers. Tag: Alexander-kin. (Author).

"Wendy Time For School", #359-1957. Bend-knee walker. Cotton dress with Venetian lace trim, straw hat with ribbon. Tag: Alexander-kin. Courtesy Bernice Heister.

"Wendy Time For School", #359-1957. Bend-knee walker. Waffle pique dress with attached large sash and Venetian lace trim. Missing straw bonnet. Tag: Alexander-kin. Courtesy Vivian Brady.

"Wendy Time For School", #359-1957. Bend-knee walker. Cotton dress with Venetian lace edging, attached large sash and straw hat with ribbon. Tag: Alexander-kin. Courtesy Vivian Brady.

"Wendy Time For School", #359-1957. Bend-knee walker. Dress in different color and material. Hat missing and flowers added. Tag: Alexander-kin. Courtesy Jay Minter.

"Wendy Fixes Tea For Company", #351-1957. Bend-knee walker. Organdy dress and dotted pinafore with one button, rickrack and braid trim. Tag: Alexander-kin. Courtesy Vivian Brady.

"Wendy After School Dress", #354-1957. Bend-knee walker. Hat goes to "Wendy Goes To Tea Party At Grandma's", #447-1956. Tag: Alexander-kin. Courtesy Lahunta McIntyre.

"Wendy After School Dress", #354-1957. Bend-knee walker. Came with various print bodices. Replaced socks and shoes. Tag: Madame Alexander/All Rights Reserved, etc. Courtesy Linda Crowsey.

"Wendy Dressed For Afternoon Tea Party", #358-1957. Bend-knee walker. Lace trimmed gingham with two buttons on front. Replaced shoes. Tag: Alexander-kin. Courtesy Linda Crowsey.

Wendy-Alexander-kins, bend-knee walkers and all mint. Left; Lavender taffeta with matching bolero, straw hat and basket of matching flowers. Matches the 1957 ''Cissy'' #2143 and ''Cissette'' #943. Middle: Yellow organdy, lace trimmed and matching straw bonnet. Green flowers at waist and green shoes, yellow socks. Right: Check taffeta, white straw hat with crimson flowers matching those at waist. Courtesy Margaret Mandel.

''Wendy Looks Pretty For School'', #360-1957. Bend-knee walker. Cotton dress with eyelet pinafore, straw hat with flowers. Replaced shoes. Tag: Alexander-kin. Courtesy Florence Phelps.

''Wendy Looks As Gay As A Buttercup'', #325-1957. Bend-knee walker. Floral polished cotton with plastron of contrasting color and two buttons. Felt hat with flowers. Doll also came with pigtails that had flowers instead of hair bows. Photo by Richard Olsen of Roosevelt-Baker Photo. Co.

"Cherry Twins", #388E-1957 Bend-knee walkers. White organdy embroidered with cherries and a cherry red hat. Tags: Alexander-kins. Courtesy Jeannie Wilson.

"School Bell Rings At Nine", #383-1957. Bend-knee walker. Cotton dress with polished cotton pinafore in a pattern with butterflies, lace over shoulders and around hem of pinafore. Flower trimmed straw hat. Tag: Alexander-kin. Courtesy Doris Richardson.

"Cherry Twin", #388E-1957. Bend-knee walker. This outfit came on a blonde and a brunette. Organdy dress with embroidered cherries and red straw hat. (Hat may be a replacement). Tag: Alexander-kin. Courtesy Pat Timmons.

"Wendy With Granny's May Basket", #365-1957. Bend-knee walker. Polished cotton with blouse of dotted Swiss and carries basket of flowers. Hairdo is rolled back on side and ribbon bow is missing. Tag: Alexander-kin. Courtesy Linda Crowsey.

"Wendy Visits With School Friend, #369-1957. Bend-knee walker. Dress buttons down back. Combination of plain and dotted organdy with attached satin "belt". Straw hat with flowers. Replaced shoes. Tag: Alexander-kin. Courtesy Florence Phelps.

"Wendy Has Many School Frocks", #368-1957. Bend-knee walker. Came in plain colors and plaid dresses. Tucked pinafore with threaded ribbon at waist. Purse added. Replaced straw hat (this one from Liesl - Sound of Music). Tag: Alexander-kin. Courtesy Florence Phelps.

"Wendy Has Many School Frocks", #368-1967. Bend-knee walker. Variation of dress which is taffeta and straw hat. Should have red shoes. Tag: Alexander-kin. Pin shown on doll was donated by the owners for a souvenir to an organization. Courtesy Marge Meisinger.

''Wendy Dressed For Trip To Market'', #382-1957. Bend-knee walker. Taffeta dress and pinafore with pinafore having lace edging. Straw hat with flowers. This outfit came in various colors. This outfit could also be a variation of #582-1956, which did come with a basket of flowers. Tag: Alexander-kin. Courtesy Loramay Wilson.

Dress from 1957. Bend-knee walker. Since these dresses are green stripe and always seem to have Holly Berries attached to waist, it would be interesting to find one in original box. Courtesy Gary Green.

''Wendy Wears Morning Dress'', #366-1957. Bend-knee walker. Floral print cotton with tie-on apron with large pocket and two buttons. Straw hat is missing. These outfits are very much like the 1955-#422 ''Helps Mummy Garden''. Courtesy Jeannie Wilson.

''Wendy Wears Morning Dress'', #366-1957. Floral print cotton dress with tie-on apron with large pocket and two buttons. Straw bonnet with flowers on sides. Courtesy Sandra Crane.

"Wendy Off To Play With Friend", #401-1957. Bend-knee walker. Lace trim. Straw hat with flowers. Red ribbons in pigtails. Tag: Alexander-kin. Courtesy Vivian Brady.

This might be variation of "Wendy Off To Play", #401-1957. Bend-knee walker. Sash ribbon added. Lavender print and deeper lavender straw hat with flowers. Tag: Alexander-kin. Courtesy Vivian Brady.

Variation of "Wendy Off To Play", #0401-1957. Bend-knee walker. Hat added. Lace on skirt forms an apron look. Tag: Alexander-kin. Courtesy Linda Crowsey.

Variation of "Wendy Off To Play", #401-1957. Bend-knee walker. Dotted organdy with lace and bow at waist. Courtesy Vivian Brady.

"Play Dress", 1957. Bend-knee walker. May be variation of #401. Hat added. Tag: Alexander-kin. Courtesy Gary Green.

"Wendy Loves To Paint", #331-1957. Bend-knee walker. Cotton dress and full pinafore that buttons down back and has two buttons on front. White straw hat with red ribbon. Tag: Alexanderkin. (Author).

"Wendy Is Fond of Morning Dresses", #345-1957. Should be on a bend-knee walker but is shown on an early straight-leg non-walker. Came in various colors and materials and open weave cloth hat with ribbon tie that matches dress. Replaced shoes and socks. Courtesy Gary Green.

"Wendy Is Fussy About School Dresses", #391-1957. Bend-knee walker. Cotton dress and pinafore. Buttons and rickrack trim. Pastel pink hat of straw with flowers at the sides. Tag: Alexander-kin. Courtesy Doris Richardson.

"Wendy Looks So Cool And Summery", #394-1957. Floral print organdy with large attached sash, and also came with satin full sash. Missing is straw hat with flowers on the sides. Replaced shoes. Courtesy Pat Timmons.

"Wendy In Suspender Dress", #392-1957. Bend-knee walker. Cotton and organdy with decorated braiding on skirt and suspenders. Felt Tyrolean hat with flowers. Replaced shoes. Tag: Alexander-kin. Courtesy Bernice Heister.

"Wendy Dance Recital", #420-1961. Bend-knee walker. Satin tutu with net skirt. Flowers in hair were originally fuller and stood up across the front of hairdo. Tag: Alexander-kins (some tagged: Wendy-kins). Courtesy Vivian Brady.

1957

"Wendy Has A Car Coat", #371-1957. Bend-knee walker. Coat is lined and she has matching slacks and bonnet. This outfit came in various colors. Tag: Alexander-kin. Courtesy Florence Phelps.

"Wendy Feels So Grown Up", #380-1957. Shows a variation of straw hat and flowers used. See doll shown below. Courtesy Jay Minter.

"Wendy Feels So Grown Up", #380-1957. Bend-knee walker. Gabardine coat over skirt and blouse. Skirt matches the coat. Straw hat with flowers and net. A different style hat is shown in the company catalog, but may have proved to be too adult for the doll. Tag: Alexander-kin. Courtesy Vivian Brady.

"Rainy Day", #373-1957. Straight-leg non-walker. Vinyl coat and "Nor' easter" hat with metal closures. Coat is lined with same material as dress. (See next photo). Tag: Alexander-kin. (Author).

Dress under "Rainy Day" set of 1957. Coat is lined with same kind and color material as the dress. Tag: Alexander-kin. (Author).

Left: "Bobby, The Boy Next Door", #347-1957. Bend-knee walkers. One-piece bodysuit of navy/red/white and felt jacket. Pressed felt cap. Right: "Wendy Dressed For Spectator Sports", #393-1957. Red top and navy pleated skirt. Felt jacket and beanie. Tags: Alexander-kins. Courtesy Florence Phelps.

"Summer Dress" shown on 1953-1954 straight-leg non-walker. Chair is from the "Start-A-Home For Alexander-kins" set of 1955-1958. Upholstered in foam rubber and covered with floral print and trimmed with fringe. This same chair came in velvet with throw pillows that match this floral print. The throw pillows for this chair and matching couch were plain velvet. Courtesy Gary Green.

''Little Minister'', #411-1957. Bend-knee walker. Small Bible attached to arm and wears chain with cross. Tag: Alexander-kin. Can also be tagged: Madame Alexander, etc. Courtesy Gary Green.

''Little Minister'', #411-1957. Has a very tiny cross and different Bible. Courtesy Margaret Mandel.

''First Communion'', #395-1957. Bend-knee walker. Organdy dress with lace ruffle and trim. Crocheted lace ''Juliet'' headpiece with tulle veil attached. Replaced shoes. Tag: Alexander-kin. Courtesy Gary Green.

This dress is often found on the ''First Communion'' doll #395-1957. Veil attached to crocheted lace ''Juliet'' headpiece. Bend-knee walker. Tag: Alexander-kin. Photo by Richard Olsen of Roosevelt-Baker Photo Co.

"Princess Anne", #393-1957. Lace dress with satin ribbon sash, straw hat with flowers. Bend-knee walkers and tagged: Alexander-kin. "Prince Charles" #397-1957. Both dolls are all original. Courtesy Roberta Lago.

"Wendy Dressed For Fun In The Sun", #315-1957. Bend-knee walker. This outfit came in plain material and in various prints. The hat also came with various styles of trim. Tag: Alexander-kin. Courtesy Florence Phelps.

"Wendy Is All Aflutter", #378-1957 variation. Bend-knee walker. Full body cotton knit suit, felt skirt and bonnet. Felt flowers on skirt and bonnet. Replaced skates, which should be boot-types. Tag: Alexander-kin. Courtesy Margaret Mandel.

"Wendy is All Aflutter", #378-1957 as shown in the catalog reprints. Bend-knee walker. Short knit bodysuit with felt skirt with attached slip, felt bonnet with flowers at the sides. Tag: Alexander-kin. Courtesy Jan Cravens.

"Infant of Prague". Bend-knee Alexander-kin. Made on special order placed by the I. Donnelly Company (a Religious article firm which operated in several large cities). Shipment was made January, 1957 and invoices indicate the order was filled during 1957. It is not positive if the arm that is bent at the elbow, and the hand that is turned were positioned at the factory, but the tiny hole in the left hand (to hold "world" globe) was done at the factory. Invoices indicate only crowns without material centers, which are basically made just like the "Queen" and "Ballerina" crowns of the 1950's with the use of plastic basing and jewels added. The plastic can be seen, or can be covered with material. The dolls were dressed by the Sisters of Mercy in Omaha, Nebraska for the I. Donnely Company. The outfits shown here are most likely made by a family member or adult with only part of original clothing (by Nuns) still with the doll. Courtesy Vivian Brady.

"Edith The Lonely Doll", #850-1958. Bend-knee walker. Character taken from book by Dare Wright which was featured in *Life* Magazine. Loop earrings and special style hairdo. Tag: Madame Alexander. Courtesy Doris Richardson.

"Wendy Wears A Bridesmaid Dress", #583-1958. Bend-knee walker. Organdy embroidered with rosebuds. Velvet sash attached at waist, lace trimmed skirt, sleeves and neck. Natural straw hat with flowers to match bouquet. Black velvet ribbon hat band. Tag: Alexander-kins. Courtesy Margaret Mandel.

"Bride", #582-1958. Bend-knee walker. "Groom" is a "Quiz-kin" of 1953-1954. Bride wears a tulle skirt with lace bodice, satin sash and chapel-style straw hat covered with tulle and flowers at sides to match the bouquet. Pearl necklace and satin (ivory color) tie-on slippers. Tag: Alexander-kins. Courtesy Margaret Mandel.

"Wendy In Party Dress", #584-1958. Bend-knee walker. Came in various pastel colors. Missing is lace bonnet which matches the gown. This outfit came boxed separately with box #16-17, and did not have the matching bonnet. The gown is nylon. Tag: Alexander-kin. Courtesy Marge Meisinger.

"Wendy Adores A Party", #566-1958. Bend-knee walker. Dotted nylon, lace trim and has large sash of same material. The flowers on hat should go completely around to the front. Tag: Alexander-kin. Courtesy Florence Phelps.

"Wendy School Days", #529-1958 and used to 1965. Bend-knee walker. Rickrack and braid trim. Pigtail ribbons tied with matching color satin ties. Came in many colors (see 1965 section). Tag: Alexander-kin. (Author).

"Wendy In Cotton Print", #531-1958. Bend-knee walker. Cotton print with rickrack trim. Felt bonnet with flower on the side. The dress is a variation of one shown in the company catalog. Replaced shoes and socks. Tag: Alexander-kin. Courtesy Jay Minter.

Boxed dress #0532-1958. Bend-knee walker. Stripe cotton with red rickrack at neck and bow at waist, white rickrack around sleeves. Tag: Alexander-kin. Dishes are 1962 Alexander as is furniture. Courtesy Linda Crowsey.

"Wendy's Morning Dress", #546-1958. Bend-knee walker. Cotton pique stripe dress, lace trim and grosgrain sash attached at waist at the bottom and crossed in front. Replaced shoes. Tag: Alexander-kin. Courtesy Florence Phelps.

"Wendy Goes To Circus", #561-1958. Bend-knee walker. Cotton dress and pinafore and white straw hat. This outfit came in various colors. Tag: Alexander-kin. Courtesy Doris Richardson.

"Wendy In Short Party Dress", #565-1958. Bend-knee walker. Outfit also came in pastel yellow. Organdy and lace with satin ribbon sash. Replaced shoes. Tag: Alexander-kin. Courtesy Florence Phelps.

"Wendy Dressed In Another Party Dress", #571-1958. Tucked organdy with lace trim, flowers at waist. Replaced hat which had flowers around top matching ones on dress. Replaced shoes and socks. Courtesy Jay Minter.

"Wendy Going To Grandmother's House," #575-1958. Bend-knee walker. Came in various colors and trim color. Replaced hat, shoes and socks. Tag: Alexander-kin. Courtesy Florence Phelps.

"Wendy As Sugar Plum Fairy", #544-1958. Bend-knee walker. Tulle and satin with matching flowers on tutu same as in hair. Tag: Alexander-kin. Courtesy Elinor Bibby.

"Wendy Ready For Devon Horse Show", #541-1958. Bend-knee walker. Navy and beige riding slacks and matching hat with bill. Navy glasses and red boots. Tag: Alexander-kin. Courtesy Marge Meisinger.

"Wendy Learning To Skate", #540-1958. Jersey leotards and long sleeve top. Felt skirt with heavy net attached. The net is shown in company catalogs, but most of these skating skirts have had the net removed by owners. Pink felt flowers on skirt. Jersey pixie cap. Courtesy Lillian Roth.

"Wendy's Rain Set", #524-1958. Bend-knee walker. Reversible rain set with bonnet lined in matching color. Metal buttons. Came with plain dress, sleeveless with lace at neck and arm holes. Replaced shoes, had cerise boots. Tag: Alexander-kin. Courtesy Florence Phelps.

Left: "Wendy Has Fun At Beach", #523-1958. Bathing suit ties in front, has embroidered flowers, matching coat, sandals and glasses. Missing sun hat with red trim. Tag: Alexanderkin. Right: "Wendy Ready To Play", #521-1958. One-piece cotton playsuit (bloomers attached). Lace trim and white sun hat with trim. Tag: Madame Alexander, etc. Courtesy Florence Phelps.

"Wendy Ready To Play", #521-1958. One-piece playsuit which appears as a short dress with flaired skirt. Bend-knee walker. Replaced shoes and socks (?). Tag: Madame Alexander, etc. Tiny bear was crafted by Marianne Gardner. Courtesy Margaret Mandel.

"Wendy In Cabana Outfit", #520-1958. Bend-knee walker. Bathing suit with tie-on skirt, sun hat and glasses. This outfit came in prints and stripes. Tag: Alexander-kin. Courtesy Linda Crowsey.

1958, 1959

The outfit on "Wendy" matches the 1958 "Cissette". "Wendy" is tagged: Alexander-kin. Material is soft jersey. Courtesy Florence Phelps.

"Wendy Goes To Garden Party", #440-1959. Bend-knee walker. Floral organdy with sash and flowers, lace hem and trim. Replaced hat. The original pale pink straw hat has matching flowers like ones at waist. Tag: Alexander-kin. Courtesy Lahunta McIntyre.

"Wendy In Flowergirl Outift", #445-1959. Bend-knee walker. Nylon gown trimmed with lace and wide satin sash. Missing is a coronet of flowers. Necklace added. This hat is style used on the "Cissette" #741-1959 "Bridesmaid", which has a pearl necklace. Tag: Alexander-kin. Courtesy Linda Crowsey.

"Wendy In Leotards Costume", #413-1959. Bend-knee walker. Pinafore has rickrack trim. Shoes are replaced and should be white with side snaps. Tag: Alexander-kin. Courtesy Vivian Brady.

116

Variation of ''Wendy In Favorite Summer Afternoon Outfit'', #444-1959. Bend-knee walker. Organdy dress and dotted Swiss pinafore with lace trim. Shoulders are ruffled instead of flat. Red straw hat, flowers missing. Tag: Alexander-kin. Courtesy Florence Phelps.

Boxed outfit #0518-1956-1959. Bend-knee walker. Dotted cotton with braid trim outlined on skirt like an apron, two bows at waist. There were variations of material and trim used over the years. Tag: Alexander-kin. Courtesy Vivian Brady.

''Wendy's'' boxed play dress of 1959-1960. Bend-knee walker. Dotted polished cotton, lace trimmed. Tag: Alexander-kin. Courtesy Billie McCabe.

''Wendy'' in boxed outfit 1959, but came on doll also. Number unknown. Bend-knee walker. Cotton gingham with wide collar trimmed with lace. Tag: Alexander-kin. Courtesy Linda Crowsey.

1959

Left: "Billy", #420-1959 and "Wendy", #432-1959. Bend-knee walkers. Tag: Alexander-kin. He wears a one-piece outfit with beanie cap. Replaced shoes, should be shoes with ties. She has one-piece skirt and blouse. Replaced panties, shoes and socks. Replaced hat and she should be wearing a beanie cap. Courtesy Bernice Heister.

Cotton gown from 1959-1962. Boxed with robe for the bend-knee walkers. Tag: Alexander-kin, Madame Alexander, etc. or Wendy-Kin. Courtesy Pat Timmons.

Unknown play dress. Ca. 1959-1961. Has much larger rickrack than what was generally used around hemline. Rickrack on bodice is normal size. Replaced shoes. Courtesy Elinor Bibby.

Unknown dress. Ca. 1959-1961. Polished cotton with wide rickrack trim, "bertha" collar with tatting-style trim. Doll is shown on a straight-leg walker but should be on a bend-knee walker. Tag: Alexander-kin. Courtesy Jay Minter.

"Wendy" of 1959 dressed in bodysuit with tie-on skirt and matching bonnet. Bend-knee walker. Tag: Alexander-kin. This outfit also came in blue and may have been available in other colors. Courtesy Christine McWilliams.

"Wendy" of 1959 dressed in variation of color. Bend-knee walker. The bonnet is missing. Purse added and replaced shoes and socks. Tag: Alexander-kin. Courtesy Jay Minter.

"Wendy Ballet" 1959 and matches the "Cissette" #713-1959. Bend-knee walker. Gold net trim around the neck with gold sequins, and tiara of gold sequins. Tag: Alexander-kins. Courtesy Vivian Brady.

"Wendy Ballet" ca. 1959. Does not have the sequins around neckline, nor the tiara of sequins. Courtesy Loramay Wilson.

1959, 1960

Left: Ballerina tutu ca. 1959. Right: #330-1960 and #420-1961. Bend-knee walkers. Tulle and satin with flowers at waist and shoulder. Should have coronet of flowers in hair. The gold ballerina's headpiece ties in back. Courtesy Marge Meisinger.

"Pink Angel", #350-1960. Bend-knee walker and tagged: Madame Alexander, etc. Taffeta gown with unlined sleeves. Gold tie shoes. Front of wings are covered with pink lace and gold metalic design, and has narrow gold braid outlining wings. Back sides of wings are plain gold foil as well as the back yoke of gown. Hair is pulled up to top of head into curls with pink roses. Photo by Richard Olsen of Roosevelt-Baker Photo Co.

"Pink Angel", #350-1960. The wings are covered in the front with gold metalic design and have narrow gold braid edging. The backs of wings are plain gold foil attached to same design yoke as in front on "Maggie" doll. Tag: Madame Alexander, etc. Courtesy Florence Phelps.

120

"Bill and Wendy Going To Circus", #320 and #332-1960. Bend-knee walkers. Tag: Alexander-kin. He wears one-piece shorts and shirt with matching cap. Tie shoes. She wears red bloomers attached to white blouse bodysuit and separate skirt. Both have bow ties. Her hat has a black ribbon band around top. Courtesy Marge Meisinger.

"Wendy Dressed In Charming Frock", #321-1960. Bend-knee walker. Variation of flowered ribbon band at hem. Tag: Alexander-kin. Courtesy Marge Meisinger.

"Wendy Dressed In Charming Frock", #321-1960. Bend-knee walker. Cotton dress with band of flowered ribbon at hem. This hairdo goes with this outfit. Purse added. Tag: Alexander-kin. Courtesy Florence Phelps.

"Wendy Dressed In Charming Frock", #321-1960. Bend-knee walker. Variation of ribbon band around hem. Hat added. Tag: Alexander-kin. Courtesy Vivian Brady.

"Wendy Looking Very Well Dressed", #340-1960. Bend-knee walker. Polished cotton and organdy with straw hat and ribbon. Purse came with outfit and is tied to wrist. Wrist tag: Wendy-kins. Courtesy Florence Phelps.

"Wendy Looking Especially Pretty", #341-1960. Bend-knee walker. This dress, pinafore and hat came in various colors. Tag: Alexander-kin. Courtesy Christine McWilliams.

"Wendy Looking Well Dressed", #340-1960. Shown on an earlier doll. Organdy top and polished cotton with matching bonnet. Buttons down back. Tag: Alexander-kin. This style dress was used for several years with last year known to be 1960. Courtesy Florence Phelps.

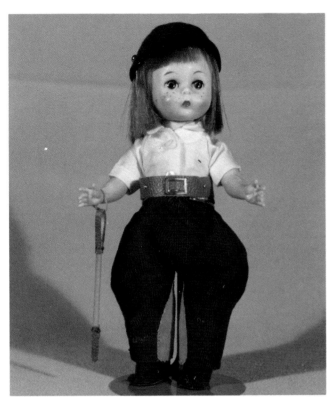

"Maggie Mixup", #0334-1960. Riding habit used also for "Wendy". Bend-knee walker. This one is tagged: Maggie. Courtesy Lillian Roth.

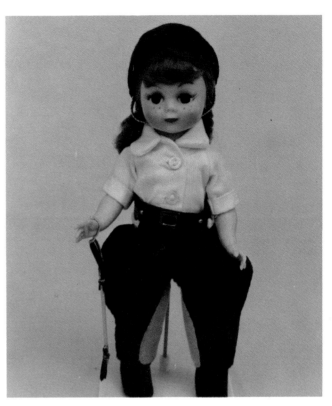

"Maggie Mixup" in riding habit used for her and for "Wendy" #0334 and #334-1960. Bend-knee walker. This Maggie has more curly bangs; red hair is in braids. Can be tagged: Maggie or Alexander-kin. Courtesy Florence Phelps.

"Maggie Mixup", #598-1960. Cotton dress and pinafore. Bend-knee walker, freckles and straight red hair. Outfit came with straw hat with flowers. Courtesy Sandra Crane.

Left: "Maggie" in #597 "Dressed For School", 1960. Pleated jumper skirt with cotton jersey top and matching sailor-style cap. Has "Wendy" face and tag. Right: "Maggie" #596 "Beach Pajamas", 1960. Two-piece and made of cotton. Bend-knee walkers. Courtesy Florence Phelps.

"Wendy Dressed For Shopping", #327-1960. Bend-knee walker. Sleeveless dress with wide collar edged with Venetian lace. Rickrack trim and white straw hat with red flowers. Watch added. Tag: Alexander-kins. Courtesy Florence Phelps.

"Dressed For School", #597-1960. On earlier doll and should be on a bend-knee walker. Also came on "Maggie Mixup". Pleated skirt, jersey top and sailor-style cap to match skirt. Top bodysuit came in short and long sleeves. Courtesy Sandra Crane.

Left: Boxed outfit #0327-1960 and right: boxed outfit #0608-1964. Courtesy Marge Meisinger.

"Wendy Dressed For Any Occasion", #335-1960. Bend-knee walker. Candy-stripe cotton dress, hemline "rolled" up and flowers are inserted on one side. Straw bonnet with wide ribbon band. Tag: Alexander-kin. Courtesy Jeannie Wilson.

Left: "Wendy Going To Circus", #332-1960. Bend-knee walker. One-piece blouse and red bloomers and plaid skirt. The little red bow tie is missing from neck of shirt. Replaced shoes and socks. Tag: Alexander-kins. Right: "Wendy Ann Trousseau" dress of 1955-#0388-1956 and #388-1957. Courtesy Joanna Brunken.

"Wendy's Coat For School" came boxed as well as coming on dolls in 1960. Hat added unless it goes with the dress the doll is wearing under the coat. Courtesy Vivian Brady.

"Maggie Mix-up" that is mint with Alexander-kin "Wendy"-style wig. Cotton gown, slippers with pompons on toes. Tag: Alexander-kin. Courtesy Jay Minter.

"Maggie Mixup" in boxed outfit 1960-1961. Bend-knee walker. Replaced shoes. Can be tagged: Maggie or Alexander-kin. Courtesy Bernice Heister.

1960-1961 "Wendy Nurse" with original navy and red cape. Bend-knee walker. Tag: Alexander-kin. Courtesy Elinor Bibby.

"Wendy Nurse" in white with baby is #429-1960-1961. The one in blue and white is #363-1962. Both have dresses and pinafores. Bend-knee walkers. Tag: Alexander-kin. Courtesy Lillian Roth.

"Maggie Mixup", 1960-1961. Bend-knee walker. Dressed in extra boxed dress for either "Wendy" or "Maggie". Courtesy Loramay Wilson.

"Maggie Mix-Up" of 1960-1961 dressed in one-piece bodysuit and wrap skirt that ties in back. Matching bonnet. The "Wendy" came dressed in this style in 1959. The outfit came in blue and may have come in other colors also. Courtesy Vivian Brady.

"Little Lady", #1050-1960. Has the "Wendy" face. Bend-knee walker. Tag: "Little Lady Doll". Is shown with various "Little Lady" toiletries. Courtesy Marge Meisinger.

"Little Lady", #1050-1960. Bend-knee walker. "Maggie Mixup" doll with straight narrow bangs and rest of hair pulled back at sides. Shown in original shadow box. Also included in the package were two packs of bubble bath, one bottle of toilet water and one bottle of perfume. Tag: "Little Lady Doll". Courtesy Lillian Roth.

Gown that came in cotton and crepe. Boxed with robe 1960-1962. Will be found on bend-knee walkers. Tag: Madame Alexander, etc. or Alexander-kins, and the tags are generally found only on the robes. Courtesy Jeannie Wilson.

Gown and robe set, 1960-1962. Will be found on bend-knee walkers. Tag: Madame Alexander, etc. Courtesy Linda Crowsey.

Robes from 1960 and have cotton gowns. Bend-knee walkers. Leatherette slippers with pompons on toes. Tag: Alexander-kin. Courtesy Florence Phelps.

"Charity Americana", #485-1961. Cotton dress with organdy blouse effect, striped socks and straw hat with wide striped band. Hair in braids with ribbons. Courtesy Gene Beckman.

"Faith Americana", #486-1961. Plaid dress with organdy blouse, straw hat and long red stockings. Hair pulled to back on top with curls. Courtesy Gene Beckman.

"Lucy Americana", #488-1961. Striped coton with organdy inset and cuffs, and white bonnet with red braid and flowers. Long white socks. Note hairdo and bangs. Courtesy Gene Beckman.

''Amanda Americana'', #489-1961. Polished cotton with organdy ruffles, buttons, braid trim and flower-trimmed hat. Striped socks and hair pulled to side in curls and tied with ribbon. Courtesy Gene Beckman.

Left: "Maggie Mixup" shown in "Wendy Bathing Set". Stretch jersey suit with cover-up coat. Tag: Alexander-kin. Ken Beckman made pail and shovel. Right: "Maggie Mixup With Watering Can", #610-1961. Overalls, shirt and sun hat. Tag: Maggie. Both are bend-knee walkers. Courtesy Gene Beckman.

"Maggie Mixup", #611-1961. One-piece leotard, pinafore with red heart and has wooden toy attached to arm. Tag: Maggie. Courtesy Roberta Lago.

Variation of costume #626-1961, "Maggie Mixup Skater". Leotards and bodysuit with felt skirt. Replaced shoe skates. Felt pixie-style bonnet. Photo by Richard Olsen of Roosevelt-Baker Photo Co.

"Anyone For Tennis?", #423-1961. Bend-knee walker. Sunsuit in one piece and wrap around, tied skirt. Came with green and red plastic tennis racket also. Tag: Alexander-kin. (Author).

"Wendy Ballet", #420-1961. Bend-knee walker. Replaced ballet slippers. Tag: Alexander-kin. (Author).

"Bride", #480-1961. Bend-knee walker. Tulle and lace with cap sleeves, coronet of flowers and tulle veil. Tag: Alexander-kin. Courtesy Sandra Crane.

"Maggie Mixup" Walking Her Dog, "Danger", #627-1961. Bend-knee walker. Cotton dress and lace trim, straw hat with flowers. Tag: Maggie, but can also be tagged: Alexander-kin. Courtesy Doris Richardson.

Left: "Maggie Mixup". Came in box as a basic doll with shoes and socks, and tagged: Maggie panties. This dress is a boxed dress from 1959 and tagged: Wendy-kin. This dress also came tagged: Alexander-kin. Hat was added. Right: Basic "Wendy". Came in box with panties tagged: Alexander-kin. Both are bend-knee walkers. Courtesy Gene Beckman.

"Maggie Mixup in Favorite School Dress", #617-1961. Bend-knee walker. Check cotton with wide sash and straw hat with ribbon trim. Tag: Maggie. Courtesy Linda Crowsey.

"Maggie Mixup Skater", #615-1961. Bend-knee walker. Cotton knit bodysuit with matching pixie-style cap with ribbon tie. Gabardine pleated skirt, grosgrain waistband. Brown leatherette shoe skates. Tag: Maggie. Courtesy Margaret Mandel.

"Maggie Angel", #618-1961. Silver yoke, wings and trim. Sleeves are lined. The wings are single in front, double in back and sewn to gown. Tag: Maggie. Courtesy Marge Meisinger.

"Maggie Angel", #618-1961. Gold yoke, trim and wings. Lined sleeves. Tag: Maggie. Courtesy Loramay Wilson.

"Wendy Dressed For Summer Day", #352-1962. Bend-knee walker. Floral print cotton dress, panties and straw hat trimmed with flowers. Tag: Wendy-kin. Courtesy Doris Richardson.

"Wendy In Party Dress", #353-1962. Trimmed with double wide and single row lace at hem. Party-style hairdo is tied with ribbon. Tag: Alexander-kin. Courtesy Linda Crowsey.

136

"Wendy In Party Dress", #354-1962. Bend-knee walker. Nylon with flowers, lace trim, and flowers on front of satin ribbon sash. Dress buttons down the back. Tag: Wendy-kin. Courtesy Linda Crowsey.

"Wendy Play Dress", #355-1962. Bend-knee walker. Cotton dress with rickrack trim. Tag: Alexander-kin. Courtesy Bernice Heister.

"Wendy Fond Of Outdoor Sports", #358. Plaid skirt, pixie-style cap matches shirt/bodysuit. Has pompon on side of cap. Also came with tie shoe roller skates. Courtesy Vivian Brady.

Outfit available from 1962-1964. Bend-knee walker. One-piece dress with pleated skirt and felt jacket with braid trim and buttons. Came as boxed set #0464-1964 with a matching bonnet hat. Tag: Madame Alexander, etc. Courtesy Linda Crowsey.

"Southern Belle", #385-1963. Bend-knee walker. Taffeta dress with lace and matching bonnet with feather plumes. Tag: Madame Alexander and also Alexander-kin. Courtesy Bernice Heister.

"Cousin Mary", #462-1963. Bend-knee walker. Organdy with lace, satin ribbon sash and matching bonnet with flower. Tag: Wendy-kin and also Alexander-kin. Courtesy Sharon Griffiths.

"Cousin Marie", #465-1963. Bend-knee walker. Polished cotton and dotted nylon pinafore, straw hat with flowers and ribbon. Tagged: Wendy-kin, also Alexander-kin. Courtesy Marge Meisinger.

"Smarty" boy and girl #1150 and #1155-1963, 12" tall. Shown are the matching "Wendy" and "Bill". Courtesy Florence Phelps.

Dress #0410-1963. Taffeta and lace. Tag: Wendy-kin. Courtesy Marge Meisinger.

"Wendy" in dress #0431-1963. Bend-knee walker. Came in taffeta and polished cotton and in various colors. Tag: Wendy-kin. Courtesy Linda Crowsey.

"Bride" and "Groom" #470 and #442-1963. Bend-knee walkers. Courtesy Marge Meisinger.

The two boys are Quiz-kins with push button on backs to shake or nod heads. Both have molded, spray painted hair, black tie shoes and are straight-leg non-walkers. The two girls are bend-knee walkers, #0464-1963 ''Spectator Sports Wendy''. Courtesy Glorya Woods.

1960's variation of #0464-1963, ''Spectator Sports Wendy''. One-piece dress with pleated skirt, felt jacket with braid trim and matching beanie with pompon. Tag: Wendy-kin and also Alexander-kin. Courtesy Marge Meisinger.

Riding outfit #0441-1963. Boxed outfit. Has pique shirt and wooden riding crop. Cap with bill and brown boots. Tag: Wendy-kin or Alexander-kin. Courtesy Marge Meisinger.

"Wendy Nurse", #460-1963. Cotton dress and pinafore. Plastic baby jointed at shoulders and hips only. Front of nurse cap should be rolled back. Tag: Wendy-kin. (Author)

1962 to 1964 Ballerina #640 and tagged: Madame Alexander, etc. Bend-knee walker. Madame Alexander chair of 1957. Courtesy Linda Crowsey.

1962-1964 Ballerina #640 and tagged: Madame Alexander, etc. Bend-knee walker. Courtesy Vivian Brady.

Wendy robe #0407 and pajamas #0405-1963. Bend-knee walker. Came with one or two rows of lace on lower legs of pajamas. Tag: Wendy-kin. Courtesy Marge Meisinger.

12″ "Janie" shown in outfit that matches the 8″ Wendy-kin and there is also a matching 18″ "Binnie" of 1964. Bend-knee walker. The 8″ outfit buttons down the back as do the large sizes. Courtesy Florence Phelps.

"Wendy Beach Outfit", #0626-1964. Boxed outfit. Bend-knee walker. Has print bloomers, terry top with applique and bows at sides. Tag: Wendy-kin. Courtesy Marge Meisinger.

"Wendy Bride", #670-1964 and #630-1965. Layers of lace on skirt and tulle with flower veil. Tag: Wendy-kin and also Alexander-kin. "Groom" is 1963. Both are bend-knee walkers. Courtesy Marge Meisinger.

Left: 1964 doll made during the time Madame Alexander was creating and making matching clothes for children under the name "Madame Alexander's Tots, Inc." There is a matching dress, as shown on this doll, for little girls. Doll is a bend-knee walker. Right: A 1953-1954 doll shown in a "School Dress" that is a jumper with bloomers of same material attached to organdy top. Right tagged: Alexander-kin and left: Wendy-kin. Courtesy Gene Beckman.

"Wendy in A-Line Dress", #673-1964. Bend-knee walker. Cotton with lace and rose applique on front of dress. Replaced shoes. Tag: Wendy-kin. Courtesy Linda Crowsey.

"Wendy Party Dress", #676-1964. Organdy dress and pinafore. Lace trimmed. Tag: Wendy-kin. Courtesy Sandra Crane.

"Wendy Ready For Party", #679-1964. Bend-knee walker. Organdy with embroidery on yoke, along with rows of lace. Pigtails with matching ribbons. Tag: Wendy-kin. Courtesy Jeannie Wilson.

Close-up of #679-1964 showing detail of the yoke embroidery. Bend-knee walker. Tag: Wendy-Kin. Courtesy Jeannie Wilson.

"Wendy Party Dress", 1964. Bend-knee walker. Wide lace forms collar and has rosette and leaves on yoke. Box reads: #400C Wendy-kins. Courtesy Loramay Wilson.

Boxed outfit of 1964. One-piece dress with pleated skirt and came in various colors. Sweater has two snaps on front with buttons sewn to front. Tag: Wendy-kin and also Alexander-kin. Courtesy Loramay Wilson.

"Play Dresses", boxed outfits #0408-1964. Came in various colors. Tags: Wendy-kins. Courtesy Marge Meisinger.

Wendy in #0619-1964 boxed dress that buttons down the back, has matching bloomers and is tagged: Wendy-kin. Courtesy Marge Meisinger.

"Wendy Riding Habit", #623-1965. Bend-knee non-walker. Tag: Wendy-kin. Courtesy Bernice Heister.

"Wendy", #622-1965. Bend-knee non-walker. Cotton dress. Hair pulled up from front into braid in back. Dress buttons down back. Tag: Wendy-kin. Courtesy Florence Phelps.

"Wendy Ballerina", #620-1965. Sequin bodice and net skirt. One-piece torso and bodice. Tag: Wendy-kin. Courtesy Vivian Brady.

"Wendy Ballerina", #620-1965. Bend-knee walker. Sequin bodice. Tag: Wendy-kin. Courtesy Marge Meisinger.

"Wendy In Organdy Dress", #621-1965. Bend-knee non-walker. Organdy and lace. Cloth flowers at waist and satin bow in hair. Tag: Wendy-Kin. Courtesy Marge Meisinger.

"Easter Doll", ca. 1966. Bend-knee walker. Tagged: Madame Alexander, etc. Egg is 8″ across and 17½″ around. Courtesy Gary Green.

"Easter Doll", ca. 1966. Bend-knee walker. Egg is 8″ tall and 17½″ around. The outfit is tagged: Madame Alexander, etc. Courtesy Lahunta McIntrye.

"Easter Doll", ca. 1966. Bend-knee walker. Egg is 8" tall and 17½" around. Outfit tagged: Madame Alexander, etc. Courtesy Florence Phelps.

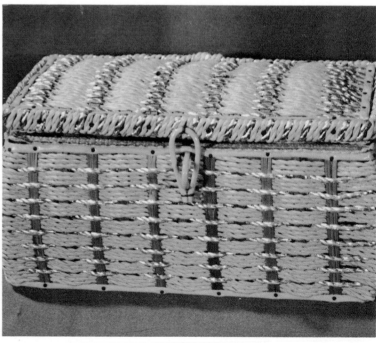

"Wendy In Sewing Basket", ca. 1966-1969. Bend-knee walker. Has pre-cut outfits to be sewn by child. Tag: Madame Alexander, etc. Courtesy Christine McWilliams.

Troupe of Ballerinas. Left: Bend-knee walker of 1966-1969. Sequin band at waist. Left brunette: 1964. Right with flowers in hair: straight-leg non-walker and dates from 1954. Longer tutu and has silk bodice with three rhinestones. Separate pink tights. Right brunette dates from 1980. Courtesy Margaret Mandel.

Yellow Ballerina that dates from 1966 to 1969. Bend-knee non-walker. Can be tagged: Madame Alexander, Wendy-kin and Alexander-kin. Courtesy Vivian Brady.

''Easter Doll'', 1968 and tagged: Madame Alexander, etc. The box is only marked: 719. Also see Miscellaneous section. Courtesy Margaret Mandel.

"Easter Doll" of 1968. Made especially for the West Coast. Only 300 of these outfits were made and came in 14" size also. Courtesy Florence Phelps.

Left: "Bride", #735-1969 to 1972. Has long straight sleeves. Right: "Bride", 1966 to 1968 with lower straight sleeves and upper arm is puff-style. Courtesy Marge Meisinger.

"Quiz-kin Groom" of 1953 is shown with "Bride" of 1970 and "Bridesmaid" of 1955. Bridesmaid has entirely different hat than the one shown in the company catalog, which is a bandeau-type covered with flowers. The flowers on this hat apparently match the ones on the front of the gown. Courtesy Roberta Lago.

Left: "The Enchanted Doll" in 1980 made for the Enchanted Doll House and a limited edition. Right: The 1981 "Enchanted Doll" which has eyelet pinafore. Both are straight-leg non-walkers. Courtesy Roberta Lago.

"Alice in Wonderland", 1953-1954. Box #365. Can be straight-leg non-walker or straight-leg walker. Tag: Alexander-kin. (Author).

The original box for "Alice in Wonderland." The price has been grease penciled out, but it can be seen lightly-$2.98.

"Alice In Wonderland". Left: #464-1955. Taffeta dress with eyelet pinafore, straight-leg walker. Right: Disneyland "Alice" of 1972. Courtesy Bernice Heister.

"Alice In Wonderland", #590-1956. Bend-knee walker. Taffeta dress with braid trim and eyelet pinafore. Rickrack around neck. Courtesy Gary Green.

''Bo Peep'', #489-1955. Taffeta gown with side panniers of floral print. Straight-leg walker. Flowers on open weave bonnet can be in middle of hat or at side as shown. There can also be a variation of the floral print. Staff is a pipe cleaner. Courtesy Bernice Heister.

''Bo Peep'', #383-1962. Bend-knee walker. Tag: Madame Alexander, etc. Plastic lamb attached with green cord that matches the ties of the wescot vest. Courtesy Lillian Roth.

Left: ''Bo Peep'' of 1962 with variation of size of plastic lamb which is tied to wrist with matching green cord of the vest. Bend-knee walker. Right: This outfit was used with a straw hat until 1973. In 1974 the hat was changed for this bonnet style. Courtesy Roberta Lago.

"Cinderella", #492-1955. Straight-leg walkers. Taffeta gowns, silver trimmed and with series of star brads. Left: Has shorter side panniers and shorter train area than doll on right. Left: Courtesy Vivian Brady. Right: Courtesy Sandra Crane.

12" and 8" "Poor Cinderella". The 12" doll is the "Lissy Cinderella" and the 8" is one never sold in stores. There are three known to exist and are referred to as prototypes. Bend-knee doll of the 1960's. The 12" is from 1966. 8" tag: Madame Alexander, etc. She wears brown suede slippers with no socks. Courtesy Gary Green.

8" "Poor Cinderella" prototype never sold to stores in the 1960's. Right: is "Cinderella", #492-1955. Straight-leg walker. Has gold trim on shoulders rather than the usual silver. Courtesy Elinor Bibby.

"Curly Locks", #472-1955. Straight-leg walker. Taffeta gown, polished cotton apron and organdy bodice. Lace cap. Courtesy Gary Green.

"Gretel", #470-1955 and "Hansel", #445-1955. Both are straight-leg walkers. She has taffeta gown and cotton floral print pinafore and bonnet. He has felt hat, velvet trousers and striped cotton stockings. Courtesy Gene Beckman.

Bend knee "Hansel and Gretel". Both were available from 1966 to 1972 with bend knees and from 1973 to date with straight legs. Tagged with their names. There can be a wide variation in the prints used. Courtesy Roberta Lago.

"Marme". All from 1955 and all are straight-leg walkers. It seems impossible there could be such a variation in costumes from one year, but since the doll, hairdo and clothes are correct we must assume this to be right. Tag: Alexander-kins "Marme". Courtesy Lillian Roth.

More variations of "Marme" of 1955. All are straight-leg walkers and have the correct hair styles. Doll on the left sitting down also came with a lavender and white striped print gown. Courtesy Lillian Roth.

"Marme". Back row left to right: 1956, thought to be 1960 and 1957. Front: All original, but not sure if she is correct or complete, nor from what year. Courtesy Lillian Roth.

"Amy". Top row left to right: 1956, 1955 and 1959. Front left to right: both are 1958 in same dress but different prints. Courtesy Lillian Roth.

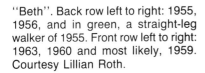

"Beth". Back row left to right: 1955, 1956, and in green, a straight-leg walker of 1955. Front row left to right: 1963, 1960 and most likely, 1959. Courtesy Lillian Roth.

"Jo". Left to right: 1959, a bend-knee walker from an unknown year, and 1955 in taffeta dress. Courtesy Lillian Roth.

"Jo". Left to right: 1956, 1960, and 1963. Courtesy Lillian Roth.

"Meg". Left to right: Possibly from the 1955 set, 1957, and maybe another from a 1955 set. Courtesy Lillian Roth.

"Meg". Back row left to right: 1957, 1960, 1955. Front row left to right: 1956, and 1958 or 1959. Courtesy Lillian Roth.

"Little Women" set from 1955. All are straight-leg walkers. Tagged: Alexanderkins along with their names such as "Marme", "Meg", etc. Courtesy Lillian Roth.

"Little Women", 1956. Bend-knee walkers. Tagged with each name. Top: Amy, Marme and Meg. Lower: Beth and Jo. Courtesy Lillian Roth.

Upper row left to right: "Jo" of 1958, "Marme" of 1960 and "Jo" of 1959. Lower row: "Amy" of 1963 and "Beth" of 1963. Courtesy Lillian Roth.

Four "Little Women" from one of the 1961 sets. Courtesy Loramay Wilson.

Set of "Little Women" along with "Laurie" of 1962. Courtesy Roberta Lago.

Set of "Little Women" of 1963. Courtesy Loramay Wilson.

Left: ''Miss Muffet'', 1965-1972 with bend knees and to date with straight legs. Center: ''Mary Mary'' from 1965 to 1972 with bend knees. 1973 to date with straight legs. Right: ''Red Riding Hood''. 1955 was dressed in taffeta, 1956 had a gown that was floor length. Came in this style from 1962 to 1972 with bend knees and from 1973 to date with straight legs. All can have a variation of prints. Courtesy Roberta Lago.

Variation of print used in dress and also the color of cup/saucer. Photo by Richard Olsen of Roosevelt-Baker Photo Co.

Shows the variation of print and apron color used for ''Mary Mary''. Photo by Richard Olsen of Roosevelt-Baker Photo Co.

"Scarlett", #485-1955. Flower print muslin, trimmed with braid and tiny bows. Sleeves are tulle and wears large straw hat with flowers. Straight-leg walker. Tag: Alexander-kin. Dark skinned doll dressed as "Mammy" with dress pulled up to show red taffeta petticoat. This doll was made up just for fun to display with "Scarlett". Courtesy Gene Beckman.

"Scarlett", #631-1956. Bend-knee walker. Floral muslin with lace trim. Braid trim at neck and on sleeves. Carries tulle parasol. Tag: Alexander-kin. Photo by Richard Olsen of Roosevelt-Baker Photo Co.

"Scarlett", #431-1957. Bend-knee walker. Two rows of ruffles of organdy and lace, red ribbon inserts to match red flowers on rayon straw hat tied with tulle bow. Medallion at neck. Tag: Alexander-kin. Courtesy Jay Minter.

Collection of "Scarletts". Upper row left to right: 1968, 1971, 1972, 1970. Two in center: 1966, 1969. Lower left: 1973 to date; center, 1956; and right, 1965. Photo by Richard Olsen of Roosevelt-Baker Photo Co.

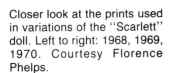

Closer look at the prints used in variations of the "Scarlett" doll. Left to right: 1968, 1969, 1970. Courtesy Florence Phelps.

Other year variations are left to right: 1967, 1972, and 1966. Courtesy Florence Phelps.

Fiction & Storybook

"Scarlett", #785-1965. Bend-knee walker and tagged: Scarlett. Gown is taffeta that came in white and ivory. Courtesy Marge Meisinger.

14", 11" and 8" "Scarlett". The 8" is from 1973 and can still be purchased. The 11" is a Cissette-Portrette of 1968 to 1973 and the 14" dates from 1968. Courtesy Gary Green.

Disney's "Snow White" and "Alice in Wonderland", 1972 to 1977. Each tagged with their name. Whether the dolls are bend-knee or the "Alex" mold straight-leg is of no consequence. Courtesy Margaret Mandel.

"McGuffy Ana", #616-1956. Bend-knee walker. Tag: Alexanderkin. Because of the doll stand pulling up the dress, and the angle from which the photo was taken, the dress appears to be much shorter than it is. The dress comes to just below the knees. Courtesy Lillian Roth.

"American Girl" 1962 to 1964 and "McGuffey", 1965, and then discontinued. Bend-knee walker and tagged with name. Courtesy Roberta Lago.

"Amish Boy & Girl". Both are bend-knee walkers and tagged with name. Made from 1966 to 1969 and then discontinued. Courtesy Roberta Lago.

"Betsy Ross". From 1967 to 1972 was bend knee, 1973 to 1975 was the "Alex" mold with straight legs and from 1976 to date is the "Alexander" mold with straight legs. Lower left is called the "Bicentennial" as this star print was used late in 1975 and into 1976. Can be on "Alex" mold or "Alexander" mold straight-leg doll. Courtesy Roberta Lago.

Left: "Colonial Girl" made from 1962 to 1964. Has deeper blue gown that is shiny and made of polished cotton. Right: "Priscilla" made from 1965 to 1970. Both are discontinued. "Colonial" is a bend-knee walker and "Priscilla" can be a bend-knee walker or a bend-knee non-walker. Courtesy Roberta Lago.

"Cowgirl and Cowboy". Both made from 1967 to 1969 and then discontinued. Both are bend-knee dolls. Courtesy Roberta Lago.

"Eskimo", made from 1967 to 1969 and then discontinued. Bend-knee doll and tagged with name. Courtesy Marge Meisinger.

"Hawaiian", made from 1966 to 1969 then discontinued. Bend-knee doll. Clothes will not be tagged. Courtesy Marge Meisinger.

"Indian Boy & Girl" made in 1966 only and will be bend-knee dolls. Name changed to "Pocahontas and Hiawatha". "Pocahontas" from 1967 to 1970, had bend-knees. "Hiawatha" from 1967 to 1969 had bend knees. Both are discontinued. Courtesy Roberta Lago.

"Pocahontas and Hiawatha". Bend knees. These dolls can have a variation of the braid trims used on the clothes, especially on the headbands. Courtesy Marge Meisinger.

"Miss U.S.A." Made from 1966 to 1968, then discontinued. Has metal crown with "jewels" and gold sandals. Has bend knees. Courtesy Roberta Lago.

"Red Boy". Made in 1972 as a bend-knee, then from 1973 to 1975 with the "Alex" marked body and straight legs, and from 1976 to date with the full "Alexander" marked body and straight legs. Photo by Richard Olsen of Roosevelt-Baker Photo Co.

"Germany". Made from 1966 to 1972 with bend knees and from 1973 to date with straight legs. Shows some of the variations of prints used for the dress and the pinafore. Courtesy Gary Green.

Variations on International Dolls

The two photos above show just a part of the different variations that were used on one doll. A very large collection could be amassed with just collecting the variations that were offered year to year. You may note in the company catalog reprints that these different prints do not show up and the reason is due to the company re-using the same photos year after year in the catalogs. The dolls in the showroom in New York City are left year after year and these different prints and variations do not even show up there.

The International and the Storybook dolls will be tagged with the name of the country they represent. International dolls can be found on bend-knee walkers, as well as the "Alex" mold straight-leg walkers of 1973 to 1976. From 1977 to date they are fully marked: "Alexander" and still have the straight legs.

There are brown-eyed dolls among the Internationals, but "Wendy Ann/Alexander-kins" did not have brown eyes.

The 8″ dolls from the "Sound of Music" set. Left to right: Gretl, Frederich and Marta. Made from 1971 to 1973 and then discontinued. Majority of these dolls have bend knees but last year of production they had straight legs using the "Alex" marked bodies. Courtesy Gary Green.

"Africa". Made from 1966 to 1971 and then discontinued. Will have bend knees. Center: "Belgium", made in 1972 with bend-knee only and from 1973 to date with straight legs. Right: "Brazil", with bend knees from 1965 to 1972 and from 1973 to date with straight legs. Courtesy Roberta Lago.

"Argentina". She was made from 1965 to 1972. He was made from 1965 to 1966. Both can be bend-knee walkers or just have the bend knees. Both are discontinued. Courtesy Roberta Lago.

Left: "Bolivia". Made from 1963 to 1966 and can be a bend-knee walker or just have bend knees. Has been discontinued. Center: "Canada". Made from 1968 to 1972 with bend knees and from 1973 to date with straight legs. Right: "Czechoslovakia". Made in 1972 with bend knees and from 1973 to date with straight legs. Courtesy Roberta Lago.

"China". Made in 1972 with bend knees and from 1973 to date with straight legs. The newer "round" face came into being after 1973. Courtesy Roberta Lago.

Left: "Denmark". From 1970 to 1972 had bend knees and from 1973 to date has straight legs. Center: "Ecuador", made from 1963 to 1966 and then discontinued. Can have just the bend knees or the early ones will be bend-knee walkers. Right: "English Guard" made from 1966 to 1968 and will have bend knees. Discontinued in 1968. Courtesy Roberta Lago.

"Dutch Boy and Girl". She was made from 1961 to 1972 as a bend-knee walker or with just bend knees. In 1973 to date the dolls came with straight legs and in 1974 began to be tagged: Netherlands. He was made from 1964 to 1972 with bend knees or as a bend-knee walker and from 1973 to date with straight legs. He began to be tagged: Netherlands, in 1974. Courtesy Roberta Lago.

"Dutch Girl". Shows early dolls using the "Wendy" and the "Maggie" heads. Both are bend-knee walkers and both carry small basket with plastic goose. Courtesy Florence Phelps.

"Greek Boy and Girl." He was made from 1965 to 1968 and then discontinued, and can be a bend-knee walker or just have bend knees. She was made from 1968 to 1972 as a bend knee and from 1973 to date as straight leg. Courtesy Roberta Lago.

"Greek Boy". Made from 1965 to 1968, then discontinued. Can be a bend-knee walker or just have bend knees. Courtesy Marge Meisinger.

This "French Flower Girl", 1956, really belongs in the Wendy Alexander-kin section but is shown here for convenience. The doll is "Wendy" dressed as a French Flowergirl in cotton gown with organdy apron, chiffon head scarf and wears white shoes with black ties. Courtesy Lillian Roth.

Left: "Finland", 1968 to 1972 as a bend-knee doll and from 1973 to date with straight legs. Center: "French", made from 1961 to 1972 and can be a bend-knee walker or have bend knees. 1973 to date doll has straight legs. Right: "Germany". Made from 1966 to 1972 with bend knees and from 1973 to date with straight legs. Courtesy Roberta Lago.

"Great Britain", made from 1977 to date and all will have straight legs. Center: "Hawaiian", made from 1966 to 1969 and then discontinued. Right: "Hungarian". Made from 1962 to 1972 and will be bend-knee walkers or just have bend knees. From 1973 to date will have straight legs. Courtesy Roberta Lago.

The very first "Hungarian of 1962 will have this headpiece which is made of braiding, rickrack and jewels. The metal headpieces were not ready until production of the 1963 dolls. Bend-knee walker. Is shown with "Italy", made from 1961 to 1963 in this outfit. In 1961, she also carried a large straw basket with flowers. From 1964 to date, there can be a great variation of materials used. Courtesy Margaret Mandel.

This metal headpiece was used on the "Hungarian" from 1963 to the late 1970's. The doll was first made in 1961 to 1965 as a bend-knee walker and from 1966 to 1972 as a bend-knee doll and from 1973 to date as a straight-leg doll. Courtesy Marge Meisinger.

Left: "India". Made from 1965 to 1972 with bend knee and as a bend-knee walker, and from 1973 to date with straight legs. Center: "Indonesia", made from 1970 to 1972 with bend knees and 1973 to date with straight legs. Right: "Ireland", made from 1964 with bend knees or bend-knee walker, and from 1973 with straight legs. Courtesy Roberta Lago.

Left: "Israeli", from 1965 to 1972 and can be a bend-knee walker or just have bend knees. 1973 to date has straight legs. Center: "Italy". Made from 1961 to 1972 and can have bend knees or be a bend-knee walker. 1973 to date has straight legs. Right: "Korea", made from 1968 to 1972 as bend knees and from 1973 to date with straight legs. Courtesy Roberta Lago.

"Japan", made from 1968 to 1972 and all will have bend knees. From 1973 to date will have straight legs. Left is a "Maggie" face and right has the newer, rounder face. Can also have the "Wendy" face. Courtesy Roberta Lago.

Americana & International

Left: "Mexico". Made from 1964 to 1972 and can have just bend knees or be a bend-knee walker. 1973 to date has straight legs. Center: "Morocco", made from 1968 to 1970 and will have bend knees. Discontinued in 1970. Right: "Norway", made from 1968 to 1972 with bend knees and from 1973 to date with straight legs. Courtesy Roberta Lago.

Left: "Peruvian Boy", made from 1965 to 1966 and can be a bend-knee walker or just have bend knees. Discontinued in 1966. Center: "Polish". Made from 1964 to 1972 with bend knees or as a bend-knee walker. 1973 to date with straight legs. Right: "Portugal", made from 1968 to 1972 with bend knees and 1973 to date with straight legs. Courtesy Roberta Lago.

Left: "Rumania". From 1968 to 1972 had bend knees and from 1973 to date has straight legs. Center: "Russia", made from 1968 to 1972 with bend knees and from 1973 to date with straight legs Right: "Scottish", from 1964 to 1972 as a bend-knee walker and just bend knees. From 1973 to date with straight legs. Courtesy Roberta Lago.

"Spanish Boy and Girl". He was made from 1964 to 1968 and then discontinued. He can be a bend-knee walker or just have bend knees. She was made from 1961 to 1972 and can be a bend-knee walker or just have bend knees. From 1973 to date she has straight legs. Courtesy Roberta Lago.

Left: "Sweden". Made from 1961 to 1972 and can be a bend-knee walker or just have bend knees. 1973 to date has straight legs. Center: "Swiss", 1961 to 1972 and can be a bend-knee walker or have just bend knees. 1973 to date has straight legs. Right: "Thailand", made from 1966 to 1972 with bend knees and from 1973 to date with straight legs. Courtesy Roberta Lago.

Left: "Turkey", made from 1968 to 1972 with bend knees and from 1973 to date with straight legs. Right: "United States", made from 1974 to date and all have straight legs. During 1974 some of the tags were misspelled to read "Untied States". Courtesy Roberta Lago.

"Tyrolean". Both made from 1966 to 1972 with bend knees and from 1973 to 1974 with straight legs. The dolls were changed in name to "Austria" in 1974, and all have straight legs. Courtesy Roberta Lago.

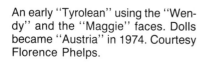

An early "Tyrolean" using the "Wendy" and the "Maggie" faces. Dolls became "Austria" in 1974. Courtesy Florence Phelps.

Left: "Yugoslavia", made from 1968 to 1972 with bend knees and from 1973 to date with straight legs. Right: "Vietnam", made in 1968 to 1969 and will have bend knees. Discontinued in 1969. Courtesy Roberta Lago.

"Scottish", used the Wendy and the Maggie faces. Can be bend-knee walker, bend knee or straight-leg non-walker. Courtesy Florence Phelps.

"Southern Mammy" (not from "Gone With The Wind") that was made up from a dark skin Alexander-kin. First place winner in "original" category at a convention. Courtesy Florence Phelps.

8″ Alexander-kin redressed in exact copy of Bridal gown worn by owner's daughter, Judy, on her wedding day. Gown made by owner, Marge Meisinger.

The doll is dressed in nylon printed with green clover blossoms and tagged: Alexander-kins. This dress was used by Marshall-Fields for St. Patricks Day with a green shamrock tied with green ribbon to wrist. Dress in green and with rose and yellow floral print was used in a trousseau case by F.A.O. Schwarz in 1955. Straight-leg walker. Did not have hat. It is not known if this case is original to the doll. Courtesy Florence Phelps.

Miscellaneous

Dining room set sold through F.A.O. Schwarz in 1957 for the 8″ dolls. Courtesy Linda Crowsey.

Dining room piece sold in 1957 through F.A.O. Schwarz. Courtesy Linda Crowsey.

Furniture sold through F.A.O. Schwarz during 1958 and 1959 for the 8″ dolls. Courtesy Linda Crowsey.

Various Wendy/Alexander-kins in different gowns and robes along with one of the wooden white beds made for the 8″ dolls. Ca. 1957. Courtesy Florence Phelps.

China tea set for the 8″ dolls and made in 1962. Came in original Alexander box that is marked #10. Courtesy Gary Green.

8″ Storyland display case showing how the 8″ dolls were used (lower front). Metal, wood and plastic. Courtesy Gary Green.

Unknown

Excellent quality Madame Alexander crown. The origin of this crown is not known. Ca. 1955-1959. Courtesy Billie McCabe.

Wendy wearing a taffeta dress with flowers at waist that match the flowers of the hat. The coat style matches the "Elise" #1640-1957, but not the material of the coat, nor the color. "Elise" also wears a pink taffeta dress under her coat. Courtesy Gary Green.

Another doll that could have items added to a basic play-style dress, such as the hat and jacket. Courtesy Florence Phelps.

It is uncertain whether or not this is a matching outfit to the #140-1962 for "Little Genius". Replaced shoes and socks. Tag: Madame Alexander, etc. Courtesy Jay Minter.

Early straight-leg walker in floral print and black straw hat. May be a match to a larger doll such as "Binnie" or "Cissy". Ca. 1955-1958. Courtesy Shirley Bertrand.

Unknown gown of organdy and lace, very much like the "Me and My Shadow" #0035E "Elaine" of 1954, which does not have the sash down the front and has a larger, flatter hat. Courtesy Gary Green.

Unknown gown of flower patterned organdy. Doll has a "Juliet" hairdo with flowers attached. Straight-leg walker. Tag: Alexanderkin. Necklace may have been added. Courtesy Florence Phelps.

Pinafore-style dress, and also known to come as a one-piece romper suit with pinafore over it. Ca. 1961-1964. Courtesy Vivian Brady.

Bridesmaid-style doll of which production is unknown. Ca. 1957-1959. Bend-knee walker. Courtesy Lahunta McIntrye.

Ca. 1960-1964. This same style dress can be dark pink with the same material as the skirt around the neck in place of the rickrack trim, also can come without the buttons in both blue and pink. Replaced shoes and socks. Shown on a bend-knee walker. Tag: Alexander-kin. Courtesy Jay Minter.

A very beautifully detailed hat and dress with unknown date, but most likely from 1960-1965. Courtesy Vivian Brady.

Unknown play dress, ca. 1956-1959. Bend-knee walker. Courtesy Elinor Bibby.

Playsuit with unknown date, ca. 1959-1960. Courtesy Vivian Brady.

"Maggie Mix-up", 1960-1961. Bend-knee walker. Dress with self-slip of organdy that has embossed design. Lace trimmed. Replaced shoes and hat added. Courtesy Jay Minter.

Very nice dress of excellent quality and all the detail of an Alexander-made outfit, although dress is not tagged. Ca. 1960-1965. Courtesy Vivian Brady.

Number Index

Index

Abbreviations

slnw....straight-leg non-walker
slw....straight-leg walker
bkw....bend-knee walker

bk....bend knee
st.l....straight leg after 1973

1956 bkw.....90	Velvet Party Dress, 1957 bkw.....93	Visitors Day At School, 1955 slw...44,45
Dress, 1955 slw.....125	Victoria, 1954 slnw.....24,27	Walks Her Dog, 1955 slw.....45
Trunk, 1956 bkw.....90	Victoria, Little, 1953 slnw.....14	Wears Polished Cotton, 1956 bkw....78
Turkey.....177	1954 slnw.....24,27	Wears Charming Ensemble, 1956 bkw.88
Tyrolean Boy & Girl.....178	Vietnam.....178	Wears Simple Dress, 1956 bkw.....79
Maggie Face.....178	Visiting Her Cousins, 1956 bkw.....78	Yugoslavia.....178
United States.....177	Visits Auntie, 1955 slw.....47	
Unknown.....182	Visits School Friends, 1957 bkw.....99	

Box Numbers on separate outfits

0327-1960.....124	0418-1955.....47	0532-1958.....112
0334-1960.....123	0425-1955.....63	0568-1956.....77
0388-1956.....48,125	0426-1955.....55	0595-1956.....58
0398-1957.....90	0431-1963.....139	0608-1964.....124
0401-1955 & 1957.....63,101,102	0441-1963.....140	0615-1955.....46
0405-1963.....141	0453-1955.....59	0619-1964.....145
0407-1963.....141	0456-1955.....57	0626-1964.....142
0408-1964.....145	0464-1964.....137,140	
0410-1963.....139	0518-1956-1959.....117	

Price Guide

Abbreviations

slnw....straight-leg non-walker
S.A.....still available
slw....straight-leg walker

bkw....bend-knee walker
bk....bend knee
st.l....straight leg after 1973

Adores A Cardigan, 1956 bkw.....325.00	1958 bkw.....325.00	Bolvia.....600.00+
Adores A Party, 1958 bkw.....325.00	1959 bkw.....365.00	Bo Peep, 1955 slw.....400.00
Agatha, 1953 slnw.....1,400.00+	1960 bkw.....275.00	1962 bkw.....195.00
Alice in Wonderland, 1954 slw....500.00+	1961 bkw.....275.00	1973 st.l.....65.00
1955 slw.....500.00	1963 bkw.....250.00	Brazil bk.....145.00
1956 bkw.....500.00	1964 bkw.....250.00	Bride, 1953 slnw.....525.00
for Disney...1972 bk or st.l.....525.00	1965 bkw.....285.00	1955 slw.....525.00
A Line Dress, 1964 bkw.....225.00	1965 yellow.....325.00	1956 bkw.....425.00
All A Flutter Skater, 1957 bkw....650.00+	1966 bk.....175.00	1958 bkw.....425.00
American Girl.....625.00	1966 yellow.....265.00	1961 bkw.....350.00
Americana, Charity, 1961 bkw...1,400.00+	1980 st.l.....S.A.	1963 bkw.....350.00
Faith, 1961 bkw.....1,400.00+	Basic Wendy, 1961 bkw.....200.00	1964 bkw.....300.00
Lucy, 1961 bkw.....1,400.00+	Basque, 1956 bkw.....385.00	1966 bk.....185.00
Amanda, 1961 bkw.....1,400.00+	Beach Outfit, 1964 bkw.....265.00	1969 bk.....165.00
Amish Boy & Girl.....550.00+	Belgium, bk.....145.00	1970 bk.....165.00
Angel, Pink, 1960 bkw.....1,900.00+	Best Man, 1955 slw.....550.00+	Bridesmaid, 1953 slnw.....700.00+
Anyone For Tennis, 1961 bkw.....325.00	Betsy Ross, bk.....150.00	1955 slw.....800.00+
Apple Annie Of Broadway, 1953 slnw.....	Bicentennial.....195.00	1956 bkw.....750.00+
.....1,400.00+	Bible Children, 1954 slnw.....	1957 bkw.....600.00+
Afternoon Tea Party, 1957 bkw.....250.00	.....2,500.00-3,200.00+	1958 bkw.....600.00+
After School Dress, 1957, bkw.....250.00	Queen Esther.....3,200.00+	Cabana Outfit, 1958 bkw.....300.00
After School, 1956 bkw.....300.00	Miriam.....2,800.00+	Calls On Grandma, 1955 slw.....345.00
Africa.....575.00+	Ruth.....2,500.00+	Calls On School Friend, 1957 bkw.325.00
Argentine Boy, bk.....500.00+	Rachael.....2,500	Canada, bk.....145.00
Argentine Girl, bk.....145.00	David.....2,500.00+	Carries Milk Money, 1956 bkw.....325.00
At Bedtime, 1955 slw.....165.00	Jacob.....2,800.00+	Charming Frock, 1960 bkw.....265.00
At Home, 1956 bkw.....300.00	Joseph.....2,500.00+	Cherry Twins, 1957 bkw.....600.00+
Attending House Party, 1956 bkw...325.00	Samuel.....2,800.00+	China, bk.....145.00
Aunt Agatha, 1957 bkw.....1,200.00+	Bill, 1955 slw.....400.00	Christening Dress, 1954 slnw....1,200.00
Aunt Pitty Pat, 1957 bkw.....1,700.00+	1957 bkw.....300.00	Cinderella Ballgown, 1955 slw...500.00+
Austria Alex. mold.....65.00	1959 bkw.....265.00	Coat For School, 1956 bkw.....250.00
Baby Angel, 1955 slw.....1,900.00+	1960 bkw.....250.00	Colonial Girl.....650.00+
Baby Clown, 1955 slw.....1,900.00+	1963 bkw.....250.00	Comes To Breakfast, 1956 bkw...300.00
Ballerina, 1953 slnw.....375.00+	Black floral pinafore outfit, slnw.....525.00	Cotton Print, 1958 bkw.....250.00
1954 slnw.....375.00+	slw.....475.00	Country Picnic, 1953 slnw....1,200.00+
1955 rose slw.....475.00+	bkw.....385.00	Cousin Grace, 1957 bkw.....1,400.00+
1956 yellow bkw.....500.00+	Blue Danube, 1954 slnw.....1,000+	Cousin Karen, 1956 bkw.....1,600.00+
1957.....375.00	Bobby, Boy Next Door, 1957 bkw.325.00+	Cousin Marie, 1963 bkw.....1,000.00+

189

Cousin Mary, 1963 bkw.......1,000.00+
Cowboy or Cowgirl.............650.00+
Curly Locks, 1955 slw.........800.00+
Czechoslvakia, bk................145.00
Davey Crockett Boy, 1955 slw...550.00+
Davey Crockett Girl, 1955 slw...650.00+
Dance Recital Ballerina, 1957 bkw..450.00
1961 bkw.....................275.00
Day At School, 1955 slw.........325.00
Day In Country, 1954 slnw.....1,400.00+
Denmark, bk......................145.00
Display Stand..................500.00+
Does The Highland Fling, 1955 slw.
........................650.00+
Does Homework, 1956 bkw.......300.00
Does The Mombo, 1955 slw......500.00
Dress For Tea Party, 1955 slw.....300.00
Dressed For Any Occasion, 1960 bkw.
.............................275.00
Dressed for Spectator Sports, 1956 bkw....
.............................300.00
Dressed in Ballgown, 1956 bkw..1,400.00+
Dressed in Oriental Influence, 1956 bkw....
.............................345.00
Dressed For June Wedding, 1956 bkw....
.........................525.00+
Dressed For Matinee, 1955 slw...325.00
Dressed For School, 1960 bkw.....225.00
Dressed For Shopping, 1960 bkw...275.00
Dressed For Summer, 1955 slw....375.00
1959 bkw.....................325.00
1962 bkw.....................385.00
Dresser, in 1953 slnw.........1,800.00+
Dude Ranch, 1955 slw..........600.00+
1956 bkw.....................600.00+
Dutch Boy or Girl, bk............145.00
Maggie Face...................225.00+
Easter, 1953 slnw.............500.00+
in egg........................1,000.00+
1968 bk.....................1,400.00+
Ecuador.......................500.00+
Edith, Lonely Doll, 1957 bkw....1,000.00+
Edwardian, Little, 1953 slnw.....1,400.00+
Enchanted Doll, 1980 & 1981....325.00
English Guard 1966-1968........500.00+
Eskimo........................650.00+
Favorite Outfit, 1953 slnw........525.00
Favorite Summer Afternoon, 1956 bkw
.........................400.00+
1957 bkw.....................325.00+
Feels So Grownup, 1957 bkw......400.00
Finland, bk......................145.00
First Communion, 1957 bkw......700.00+
First Long Dancing Dress, 1956 bkw....
.............................600.00
First Sailor Dress, 1956 bkw.......485.00
Fixes Tea For Company, 1957 bkw.325.00
Flowergirl, 1956 bkw............600.00+
Short Dress, 1956 bkw........365.00+
1959 bkw.....................500.00+
Fond Of Morning Dress, 1957 bkw..250.00
Fond of Outdoor Sports, 1962 bkw..275.00
French, bk.......................145.00
French Flowergirl, 1956, bkw.....550.00+
Fun At Beach, 1958 bkw.........325.00
Fun In The Sun, 1957 bkw........275.00
Fun Wearing Black Pinafores, 1956 bkw....
.............................325.00
Fussy About School Dresses, 1957 bkw....
.............................325,00
Garden Party, 1953 slw.......1,200.00
1955 slw.....................800.00+
1956 bkw.....................600.00+
1959 bkw.....................450.00+
Gay As A Buttercup, 1957 bkw....275.00
Germany, bk.....................145.00
Goes To Ballet, 1956 bkw........600.00+
Goes Calling With Mother, 1956 bkw......
.............................325.00

Goes To Circus, 1958, bkw........325.00
1960 bkw.....................285.00
Goes Ice Skating, 1956 bkw.....650.00+
Goes Marketing, 1955 slw........265.00
Goes Roller Skating, 1955 slw....650.00+
Goes To Matinee, 1955, slw......325.00
Goes To School, 1953 slnw........325.00+
1956 bkw.....................300.00+
Goes To Sunday School, 1955 slw...325.00
1956 bkw.....................300.00
Goes On Train Journey, 1955 slw....335.00
Goes Walking, 1956 bkw.........325.00
Goes Visiting, 1955 slw.........345.00
Going To Grandmother's House, 1958 bkw..
.............................265.00
Going with Mother, 1955 slw......425.00
Godey, Little, 1954 slnw......1,000.00+
Godey Lady, 1955 slw.........1,000.00+
Good At Tennis, 1955 slw........400.00
Gown, Night, 1954 slnw.........200.00
1955 slw.....................165.00
1956 bkw.....................165.00
1958 bkw.....................165.00
1959 bkw.....................150.00
1960 bkw.....................150.00
Graduation, 1957 bkw........1,200.00+
Grandma Comes To Tea, 1955 slw..295.00
Granny's May Basket, 1957 bkw...265.00
Great Britian...................S.A.
Greek Boy.....................500.00+
Greek Girl, bk...................145.00
Gretel, 1955 slw..............900.00+
1966 bk.....................165.00+
Groom, 1953 slnw.............675.00+
1956 bkw.....................550.00+
1957 bkw.....................550.00+
1963 bkw.....................500.00+
1965 bkw.....................450.00+
Guardian Angel, 1954 slnw.....1,600.00+
Hansel, 1955 slw..............900.00+
1966 bk.....................165.00+
Has A Car Coat, 1957 bkw.......400.00
Has Many School Frocks, 1957 bkw..325.00
Hawaiian......................525.00+
Helps Cutting Flowers, 1955 slw...325.00
Helps Mummy, 1955 slw.........300.00
Helps Mummy Garden, 1955 slw...300.00
Hiawatha.......................500.00
Highland Fling, 195 slw........650.00+
Hungarian, bk....................145.00
India, bk.......................145.00
Indian Boy & Girl.............500.00+
Indonesia, bk....................145.00
Infant of Prague.............1,800.00+
Interesting Dress From Wardrobe, 1956 bkw
.............................300.00
Invites Guest To Lunch, 1956 bkw...300.00
Ireland, bk......................145.00
Israeli, bk.......................145.00
Italy, bk........................145.00
Japan, bk.......................145.00
Janie, 1964....................350.00
Juliet, 1955 slw..............1,800.00+
Jumper Outfit, 1953 slnw........425.00
1954 slnw....................425.00
June Wedding, 1956 bkw........525.00+
Korea.........................475.00+
Lady In Waiting, 1955 slw.....1,600.00+
Learning To Skate, 1958 bkw.....500.00+
Leotards, 1959 bkw.............275.00
Likes a Rainy Day, 1955 slw.....325.00
Little Lady, 1960 bkw...........850.00+
Wendy Face, 1960 bkw.......700.00+
Little Women, 1955 slw........225.00 each
1956 bkw.....................175.00 each
1958 bkw.....................175.00 each
1959 bkw.....................175.00 each
1960 bkw.....................125.00 each
1961 bkw.....................125.00 each

1962 bkw.....................125.00 each
1963 bkw.....................125.00 each
Looking Especially Pretty, 1960 bkw.....
.............................325.00
Looking Well Dressed, 1960 bkw..325.00
Looks Cool and Summery, 1957 bkw...
.............................275.00
Looks Pretty For School, 1957 bkw....
.........................250.00+
Looks Sweet As Lollipop, 1956 bkw200.00
Loves Cardigans, 1955 slw.......365.00
Loves Pinafores, 1955 slw.......295.00
Loves School Dress, 1955 slw....225.00+
1957 bkw.....................300.00
Loves To Paint, 1957 bkw........300.00
Loves To Swim, 1955 slw........325.00
Loves To Waltz, 1955 slw........600.00
Madaline, 1953 slnw...........650.00+
1954, Neiman-Marcus slnw....575.00+
Maggie Mixup, 1960-1961 bkw..450.00+
Angel, 1960 pink bkw.......1,900.00+
Angel, 1961 bkw...........1,900.00+
Beach Pajamas, 1960 bkw......450.00
Dress, 1960 bkw..............450.00
Favorite School Dress, 1961 bkw550.00
Ice Skater, 1961 bkw.........600.00
Pants & Top, 1960 bkw........450.00
Riding Outfit, 1960 bkw......600.00
Robe or night gown...........450.00
Roller Skating, 1961 bkw......600.00
Skirt/body suit, 1960 bkw.....450.00
Skirt/shirt, 1960 bkw........450.00
Walking Her Dog, 1961 bkw...600.00
Wendy Face, 1960 bkw.......450.00+
With Watering Can, 1961 bkw..600.00
With Wooden Toy, 1961 bkw..500.00
Majorette Costume, 1955 slw..1,400.00+
Mary Louise, 1954 slnw......1,000.00+
Mary, Mary, bk.................165.00
Maypole Dance, 1954 slnw.....475.00+
1955 slw.....................425.00+
McGuffey, 1956 bkw..........1,000.00+
1965 bk.....................600.00+
Melanie, 1956 bkw...........1,400.00+
Mexico, bk.....................145.00
Minister, Little, 1957 bkw....1,600.00+
Miss Muffet, bk.................165.00
Miss U.S.A....................325.00
Morning Dress, 1957 bkw........300.00
1958 bkw.....................265.00
Morocco.......................500.00+
Nana Governess, 1957 bkw...2,000.00+
Needs More Than One Coat, 1956
bkw.........................325.00
Neiman-Marcus, 1953 slnw....650.00+
1954 slnw....................575.00+
1955 slw.....................575.00+
Netherland Boy or Girl, Alex. mold..65.00
Norway, bk.....................145.00
Nurse, 1956 bkw...............950.00+
1960 bkw.....................900.00
1960 with cape...............900.00+
1963 bkw.....................900.00+
Off To Play With Friends, 1957 bkw265.00
Off On Shopping Jount, 1956 bkw.325.00
Off To See Grandma, 1956 bkw...345.00
On A Hot Morning, 1956 bkw.....300.00
On School Trip, 1956 bkw.......325.00
On Way To Beach, 1955 slw......325.00
1956 bkw.....................300.00
Organdy dress, 1965 bkw........250.00
Oriental Influence, 1956 bkw.....345.00
Outfit For Rainy Day, 1955 slw....325.00
Pajamas, 1953 slnw.............200.00
1956 bkw.....................165.00
1963 bkw.....................150.00
Parlour Maid, 1956 bkw........1,800.00+
Party Sun Dress, 1957 bkw........300.00
Dress, 1958 bkw..............400.00

Dress, Short 1958 bkw...........250.00
Dress, 1962 bkw..............200.00
1964 bkw.................265.00
Perky Hairdo, 1956 bkw.........300.00
Peruvian Boy..................525.00 +
Peter Pan, 1953 slnw.........1,400.00 +
Pierrot Clown, 1956 bkw......1,600.00 +
Plans Shopping Trip with Grandma, 1955
    slw...................395.00
Play Dress, 1955 slw..............325.00
    1957 bkw.................300.00
    1959 bkw.................225.00
    1962 bkw.................185.00
    1964 bkw.................165.00
Plays On Beach, 1955 slw.........325.00
Plays in Garden, 1955 slw.......325.00
Plays Tennis, 1956 bkw.........400.00
Playsuit, 1956 bkw.............275.00
Pocahontas..................500.00 +
Polish, bk...................145.00
Portugal, bk..................145.00
Prettiest Girl, 1955 slw.........325.00
Prince Charles, 1957 bkw.......1,000.00 +
Princess Anne, 1957 bkw.......1,000.00 +
Priscilla...................650.00 +
Rain Set, 1956 bkw.............325.00
    1958 bkw.................325.00
Rainy Day, 1953 slnw...........475.00
    1955 slw.................325.00
Ready For Any Weather, 1956 bkw........
    ....350.00
Ready For Devon Horse Show, 1958 bkw...
    ....500.00 +
Ready for Garden Party, 1955 slw......
    ....800.00 +
Ready For Opera, 1955 slw.......600.00 +
Ready For Party, 1955 slw.........325.00
    1964 bkw.................265.00
Ready For Plane Trip, 1955 slw....350.00
Ready To Play, 1958 bkw.........300.00
Ready for Stroll in Park, 1955 slw...325.00
Red Boy, bk..................185.00
Red Riding Hood, bk.............165.00
Rides Well, 1956 bkw...........450.00 +
Riding Outfit, 1963 bkw.........300.00
    1965 bkw.................300.00
Robe, 1955 slw...............165.00
    1958 bkw.................165.00
    1960 bkw.................150.00
Rodeo, 1955 slw.............1,800.00 +

Roller Skating, 1955 slw.........650.00 +
    1956 bkw.................650.00 +
Romeo, 1955 slw.............1,800.00 +
Rumania, bk..................145.00
Runs To Market, 1956 bkw........345.00
Russia, bk...................145.00
Queen, 1954 slnw.............600.00 +
    1955 slw.................600.00 +
Quizkin, 1953 slnw...........1,200.00
    1954 slnw...............1,200.00
Scarlett, 1955 slw...........950.00 +
    1956 bkw...............950.00 +
    1957 bkw.............1,100.00 +
    1965 bkw.................600.00 +
    1966 bk..................600.00 +
    1967 bk..................600.00 +
    1968 bk..................600.00 +
    1969 bk..................600.00 +
    1970 bk..................600.00 +
    1971 bk..................600.00 +
    1972 bk..................600.00 +
    1973 bk..................165.00
School Bell Rings at Nine, 1957 bkw.......
    ....325.00
School Coat, 1955 slw...........300.00
School Dress, 1953 slnw.........325.00 +
    1955 slw.................325.00 +
    1956 bkw.................300.00
    1957 bkw.................250.00 +
    1958 bkw.................250.00 +
    1960 bkw.................225.00
    1964 bkw.................200.00 +
School Trip, 1956 bkw...........325.00
Scottish, bk..................145.00
Sewing Basket, 1966..........1,200.00 +
Shopping With Auntie, 1954 slnw....465.00
Slip, 1954 slnw................20.00
Smart School Outfit, 1955 slw.....325.00 +
Smarty, 1963.................350.00
Snow White, Disney.............685.00 +
So Dressed Up, 1954 slnw & slw..675.00 +
Sound Of Music Gretl.............195.00
    Frederich................195.00
    Marta...................195.00
Southern Belle types, 1954 slnw.1,000.00 +
    1955 slw.................600.00
    1956 in pink bkw.........1,000.00 +
    1956 in blue bkw..........$1,000.00 +
    1963 bkw.................700.00 +
Southern Girl, Little, 1953 slnw..1,200.00 +

Spanish Boy.................465.00 +
    girl bk...................200.00
Spectator Sports, 1956 bkw.....300.00
    1963 bkw.................275.00
Spring Holiday, 1954 slnw.......485.00
Story Princess, 1956 bkw.....1,400.00 +
Stroll In Park, 1955 slw.........325.00
Sugar Plum Fairy, 1958 bkw.....325.00
Summer Dress, 1957 bkw.......250.00
Sunday Breakfast, 1956 bkw.....325.00
Sunday School Dress, 1954 slnw..425.00
    1955 slw.................325.00
Sunsuit, 1954 slnw............425.00
    1955 slw.................325.00
Suspender Dress, 1957 bkw.....285.00
Sweden, bk...................145.00
Swedish, bk..................145.00
Takes Fruit To Grandma, 1956 bkw345.00
Tea Set.....................65.00
Tennis, 1956 bkw.............400.00
Toddler, 1955 slw.............400.00
Thailand, bk..................145.00
Time For School, 1957 bkw.......300.00
Travel Trunk, 1956 bkw single...500.00 +
    double..................850.00 +
Trip To Market, 1956 bkw.......345.00
    1957 bkw.................325.00
Trousseau, 1953 slnw.........800.00 +
    Case, 1955 slw..........1,000.00 +
    Dress, 1955 slw.........300.00
Turkey, bk...................145.00
Tyrolean Boy or Girl, bk.........145.00
    Maggie Face..............225.00 +
United States, Alex. mold........130.00
Velvet Party Dress, 1957 bkw.....400.00
Victoria, 1954 slnw..........1,200.00 +
Victoria, Little, 1953 slnw.....1,200.00 +
    1954 slnw...............800.00 +
Vietnam....................525.00 +
Visiting Her Cousins, 1956 bkw...300.00
Visits Auntie, 1955 slw.........345.00
Visits School Friends, 1957 bkw...285.00
Visitors Day At School, 1955 slw..325.00
Walks Her Dog, 1955 slw........325.00
Wears Polished Cotton, 1956 bkw.375.00
Wears Charming Ensemble, 1956
    bkw....................400.00
Wears Morning Dress, 1957 bkw..300.00
Wears Simple Dress, 1956 bkw...300.00
Yugoslavia, bk................145.00

Two Important Tools For The
Astute Antique Dealer, Collector and Investor

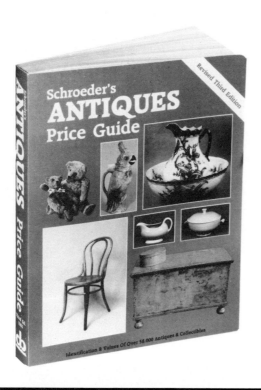